Bomber offensive: the devastation of Europe

D0374606

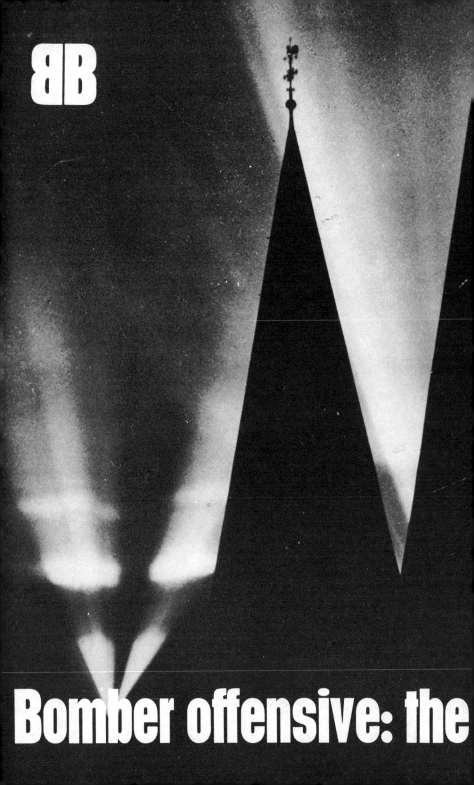

BB

Bomber offensive: the

Noble Frankland

devastation of Europe

Editor-in-Chief: Barrie Pitt
Art Director: Peter Dunbar

Military Consultant: Sir Basil Liddell Hart
Picture Editor: Robert Hunt

Executive Editor: David Mason
Designer: Sarah Kingham
Special Drawings: John Batchelor
Cartographer: Richard Natkiel
Cover: Denis Piper
Research Assistant: Yvonne Marsh

Contents

Reaping the whirlwind

Introduction by Barrie Pitt

In the high summer of 1940, rather more than three thousand gallant young men saved Britain from invasion and perhaps the whole world from an evil domination. Their example fired the imagination of a generation and what was rightly called the cream of Britain's youth flocked to join the Royal Air Force – to find, the majority of them, that there was not so great a demand as they had hoped, for an expansion of Fighter Command, which had won so glorious a place in history in the Battle of Britain.

No matter; it was time anyway to turn from defence to attack.

'We shall bomb Germany,' Churchill had said, 'by day as well as by night in ever-increasing measure, casting upon them month by month a heavier discharge of bombs, and making the German people taste and gulp each month a sharper dose of the miseries they have showered upon mankind.'

Bomber Command carried the war to the enemy – indeed, for many crucial months it constituted the only arm by which Britain could demon-strate to the world that she had not capitulated to Hitler in the same manner as had her ally France. The crews that flew the Hampdens, Whitleys and Wellingtons, and later the Stirlings, Halifaxes and Lancas-ters, through the night skies above Europe, carried with them not only menace to the aggressor, but also the self-respect and growing confidence of their own countrymen.

Dr Noble Frankland is one of the most distinguished historians writing today and, moreover, served himself in Bomber Command as a navigator. He was also joint author, with Sir Charles Webster, of the official history 'The Strategic Air Offensive against Germany 1939–1945' written while serving as an official historian in the British Cabinet Office. Nobody knows more of the course of the campaign which has become known as the Bomber Offensive against Germany, and few historians have his ability to present so intricate and controversial a story in so lucid and persuasive a manner as he has done here.

For the story of that Bombing Offensive is by no means a straightforward account of growing power in the air slowly but steadily crushing the industrial potential of the enemy, or even of dismaying the enemy population. By 1941 it was realised that the level of technical sophistication in bombing techniques was hardly enough to ensure that bombs landed within five miles of their targets, even when the rudimentary navigational techniques took the bombers over the right towns. Crucial scientific advances had to be made, decisions of imagination and courage taken, battles of wits and ingenuity fought, before the aims of those who directed the offensive came within striking distance.

By the time Bomber Command was joined in the growing battle by the United States Eighth Air Force, much had been accomplished – but then much had also been accomplished by German scientists and airmen in perfecting their system of air defence. Dr Frankland's fascinating account of the ebb and flow of battle as one technical advance would give one side or the other some temporary advantage or respite, constitutes one of the most valuable lessons to be learned from his book.

But with the advent of the Americans, the battle of course grew enormously in scope – and in human cost. The extraordinary devotion to duty of the men who flew the bombers is indicated by the fact that more awards and decorations were won by them, than by the men of any other arm – and more cruelly by the fact that of the men who died, over 25,000 have no known grave. That many died in the early days without themselves having inflicted much more than discomfort on the enemy is undeniable, for they had not the weapons to do more; but their experience and their very needs led eventually to the provision of equipment of a standard to match their courage.

The background

The conquest of the air gradually led the military and naval staffs of the great powers, which were then drifting towards Armageddon, to consider what application the new flying machines, aeroplanes, sea planes and airships, might have over the battlefield and the naval actions. The first and most obvious consideration was that aviators would be able to see farther than cavalry or staff officers surveying the countryside from horseback or hill tops. So the original role of air power in war was one of reconnaissance. Tentative experiments took place both in military exercises and in some of the fighting actions which preceded the outbreak of general war in August 1914. Thereafter three developments of the original reconnaissance idea rapidly occurred.

First, if aeroplanes could survey the immediate environs of the battlefield or potential fleet action, the longer range ones could also see what was going on behind the lines or in the naval bases. This activity came later to be known as 'strategic' reconnaissance. Secondly, while it was advantageous to obtain such information oneself, it was also desirable to try to deny it to the enemy and from this sprang the idea and the actuality of

air combat, in which aircraft engaged each other first with handarms and then with machine guns. Thirdly, if aircraft or airships could pass over the enemy lines to survey their troops, fortifications, entrenchments and back areas behind the lines, they could also drop explosives upon them. From this developed the practice of bombing.

Like reconnaissance, bombing had from almost the outset two distinctive applications. One was tactical in the sense that the attacks would be on the forces immediately in the battle areas and would be part of the battle itself. The other was strategic

An Avro bomber in 1914. This was an early form of the famous Avro 504

in the sense that the attacks would be on the bases or supporting facilities behind the lines from which the enemy drew his armed strength. Another way of expressing the same distinction is to say that tactical bombing was largely concerned with the manifestations of the enemy's armed strength and strategic bombing with its sources.

Even this last idea, that of strategic bombing, which, because it tended to involve longer flights than the other ideas, was the most advanced appli-

9

cation of air power, found some expression almost from the outset of the First World War. The British Royal Naval Air Service towards the end of 1914 made bombing attacks, aimed mainly at Zeppelin sheds, as far from the battlefield as Cologne and Düsseldorf. The Germans similarly raided Dover and Erith. Subsequently there was a great extension of these small beginnings by both sides, but especially by the Germans. They had a marked lead in the development of airships and, in January 1915, they employed them to initiate the first systematic and sustained strategic air offensive in history. In the course of the war, these airships dropped nearly 200 tons of bombs and killed some 550 people. They started at Yarmouth during the night of 19th-20th January 1915 and reached London for the first time on that of 31st May-1st June.

These operations, though they scarcely affected the course of the war, did, through their very novelty, make a considerable impression. They also evoked opposition which in the course of 1916 revealed that Zeppelins were fairly easy targets for 'fighter' aeroplanes or even anti-aircraft guns.

Zeppelin L 11 in 1915

They were large, slow moving and highly inflammable. Their losses became, for the Germans, very serious and new methods of maintaining the attack had to be thought up. These found expression early in 1917 in the invention by the Germans of a long range bomber force equipped with Gothas, the first authentic heavy bomber aircraft. From what the Germans sowed in these bombing operations they eventually, in the fullness of time, reaped the whirlwind, for it was from the Gotha attacks that in Britain there sprang, as a reaction, in 1918 the Royal Air Force and in 1936 Bomber Command.

The attacks by Gothas, which were sometimes accompanied by Giants, began in April and gradually extended until on 13th June 1917 an action of the greatest historical importance took place. This consisted of a daylight attack on London by fourteen Gothas which dropped 118 bombs and killed 160 people. Nearly one hundred British 'fighters' tried to ward off the attack but they claimed not a single victim; all the Gothas returned safely to their bases. It seemed as though London lay at the mercy of the German bomber force. If a mere fourteen of their number could achieve such results in broad daylight without any loss at all to themselves what did the future portend? This was the question in the minds of an outraged populace and an alarmed government, the government of Mr Lloyd George. To answer it, an Imperial statesman, General Smuts, was called in.

He reckoned that air power had introduced, through its capacity for this sort of bombing, an entirely new dimension in the conduct of war. He even thought it likely that this kind of warfare would prove to be so powerful that the older forms of military and naval actions would become 'secondary and subordinate'. Smuts made various recommendations designed to improve the air defence against these bombing attacks, but the essence of his opinion was that the only real defence was counterattack and Smuts called for the rapid development of a British bombing force to attack Germany. These air operations, Smuts believed, would require special study and direction. They were not an extension of military and naval methods. They were a new kind of war. They would need to be planned by a specialised staff and carried out by a special service. Smuts therefore recommended the creation not simply of an 'independent' bomber force, like the German one, but also of a separate Air Staff and a new and separate fighting service. His recommendations were immediately accepted and rapidly translated into action. In October 1917 a wing was formed at Ochey for the special purpose of long range bombing of German targets. On 1st April 1918 the Royal Air Force came into being as the first separate fighting air service in the world. In June 1918, from the basis of the Ochey Wing, which had subsequently become the VIII Brigade, there was formed the Independent Force which was to mount a strategic bombing offensive against Germany 'independently' of the land and sea campaigns which had previously absorbed nearly all Britain's air power.

By the time this had happened, the Gothas and Giants had been substantially contained by the improved air defences. Though not as vulnerable as airships, these relatively heavy aircraft found it hard to compéte in the face of the much lighter fighters which came up to intercept them. Increasingly these took to night action which also had its hazards. Of the sixty Gothas and Giants lost in operations in 1917 and 1918, thirty-six came to grief in crashes at their own bases in Belgium on returning from England. Nor did the operations of the Ochey Wing, the VIII Brigade or the Independent Force amount to enough to prove or disprove Smuts's predictions. The V1500

Handley Page four-engined heavy bomber which was to have a range sufficient to reach Berlin from British bases and power enough to lift a bomb load of more than 3,000lb, had not come into service when the older form of military operations brought the war to an end in November 1918. It seemed that the new Royal Air Force and, in particular, the Independent Force, had missed the bus and that General Smuts's proclamation of the advent of a strategic revolution might quickly be forgotten. This, however, was not to be.

In Britain there arose the extraordinary and dominating figure of Trenchard who for ten years was Chief of the Air Staff and for years after that the presiding genius of the Royal Air Force. The Trenchard doctrine was based on Smuts. It proclaimed that in air war, the best defence was counterattack. It also laid down that the moral effect of bombing would prove to be much more effective than the physical and that in a future war the way to victory lay through the development of a heavier bombing offensive against the heart of the enemy than the enemy could bring to bear against one's own heart. Since there was, according to the Trenchard doctrine, no direct defence against bombing, the air force should concentrate its efforts upon the creation of a bombing force. Fighters were no more than a sop to civilians and politicians. Air superiority would consist in being able to lift a greater weight of bombs more readily than the enemy.

Trenchard did not succeed in creating forces with much actual capacity for carrying out such ideas in war, nor did he inspire the air force of which he was for so long the professional head, with either an enquiring or an experimental frame of mind. The operational problems of bombing such as target finding, bomb aiming and even ordinary navigation were, indeed, virtually ignored and, to a considerable extent, not even recognised.

Trenchard, however, did succeed in keeping the Royal Air Force in being and in preserving the idea of a strategic air offensive as its main role. This was a considerable feat which perhaps no other man could have achieved.

In Germany, where the idea of strategic bombing had grown so fast during the First World War, it declined almost equally precipitately in the inter-war years. Experience in the Spanish Civil War suggested to the Luftwaffe that the most effective employment of aircraft was the direct support of the army in the field and since the Germans were aiming at victory through military strength in the narrow sense of their army, this was not a surprising conclusion. General Wever, the first Chief of Staff of the restored Luftwaffe, who advocated the construction of a heavy long range bomber force, was killed in a flying accident in 1936 at Dresden. His death may well have saved Britain from much destruction and suffering. When war came, the Germans had no systematic plans for a strategic air offensive against Britain and, by comparison with the extent to which other branches of their armed forces were developed, a bomber force of unimpressive quality.

Though Italy lacked the economic independence to vie with the great powers in the development of air power or other military expressions, she did produce a General, Giulio Douhet, who, through his writings, exercised a remarkable influence upon the doctrines of air power. Douhet believed that future wars would be determined by air power alone. He more than endorsed Smuts's prediction. He thought that military and naval operations would be not merely secondary and subordinate but irrelevant. He suggested that the decisive campaign would be the long range bomber offensive which by striking massive blows at the very heartland of the enemy would rapidly reduce his cities to ruins, his people to despair and his government to capitu-

Above: Gotha bomber. *Below:* Handley Page V1500 bomber

Trenchard

Sir Arthur Harris

Smuts

lation. As the instrument of this offensive, Douhet envisaged a battle plane or armed bomber which would fight its way to the target. Thus, like Trenchard, Douhet believed that the decisive point of action was against the enemy people themselves and that the capital weapon for exploiting the opportunity for victory through the moral collapse of the enemy was the bomber.

The extent to which Douhet directly inspired the development of air doctrine in Britain and the United States is a point of some controversy but it cannot be doubted that his ideas gained a general currency which both reflected and helped to form opinion. Some have seen in the design of the B17 which eventually became the main instrument of the American bombing offensive against Germany, the reflection of Douhet's battle plane. Moreover, the Americans did plan to send these battle planes into action without fighter cover in self-defending formations though it may be argued that the apparently insoluble problem of a long range fighter was a more important factor in that design than the writings of Douhet.

Even so, the main influence upon American bombing doctrine was the reaction to British precept and, after the outbreak of war, the British practice in the early stage of the Bomber Command offensive against Germany. This reaction was sympathetic in the sense that it resulted in a strongly pronounced belief in the theory of a strategic bombing offensive and the specification and ordering of two four-engined types which became the B17 Flying Fortress and the B24 Liberator. The reaction was unsympathetic in the sense that the Americans were unimpressed by the British concept of night area bombing. The Americans pinned their faith much more exclusively than the British to precision attacks in daylight.

The British doctrine of bombing which moulded the course of the

Bomber Command offensive and influenced that of the American equivalent was not, however, quite the Trenchard doctrine. In the last years of peace, when Sir Cyril Newall was Chief of the British Air Staff and Neville Chamberlain Prime Minister, important qualifications of Trenchard's doctrine were introduced. These were due partly to the need to face the realities of an increasingly grim situation and partly to scientific and technical developments. Exaggerated fears of the moral effect of bombing, a legacy of the Trenchard doctrine and the Douhet philosophy, also played an important formative part.

The realities of the situation were that in the forthcoming war, despite Britain's rearmament programme and despite the size of the French army, the Germans would start at a moment of their own choice, in a theatre selected by them, and with a pronounced military superiority. It also seemed that they would start with an alarming air superiority and there was in Britain, not only in the newspapers or the popular imagination, but also in the Air Staff, a real fear that German bombers might strike at Britain in general and London in particular a 'knockout blow' which would cause such grotesque destruction, death and suffering as to make the continuance of the war impossible.

The solution posed by the Smuts prediction, the Trenchard doctrine and the Douhet philosophy alike, had been to build a superior bomber force for stronger counterattack and this too had, at least in theory, been the government's solution. It had in 1932 been enshrined in the famous observation made in the House of Commons by the Prime Minister, Baldwin, to the effect that the bomber will always get through and that therefore the only defence was counterattack. After 1936, however, when Bomber Command was formed, it increasingly became apparent that Britain simply could not clothe this theoretical solution

with the actual weapons required. A test mobilisation of Bomber Command during the Munich crisis showed starkly that it was not ready to go effectively into action. Even a year later, its still comparatively new Wellingtons, Whitleys and Hampdens were neither sufficiently numerous nor adequately worked up and equipped to mount a serious bombing offensive.

Thus, though the Air Staff continued to pay lip service to the Trenchard doctrine and to hope for its practical revival when the four-engined bombers, which were specified in 1936, came along in 1940 or 1941, they were in the meantime compelled to depend upon air defence. When they wavered, the government insisted and it was, in fact, the civilian minister for the Coordination of Defence, Sir Thomas Inskip, who insisted in 1937 and 1938, on priority being given not to Bomber but to Fighter Command.

So between 1937 and 1940 there was developed in Britain not, as theory would have suggested, the strongest bomber force, but the most advanced system of air defence in the world. Fighter Command was equipped with Sydney Camm's Hawker Hurricane and the yet more impressive Supermarine Spitfire designed by R J Mitchell. The problem of how to bring these splendid aircraft to the correct points of interception so that they could bring their performance and fire-power to bear upon attacking enemy air forces was solved by the invention, designing and operational working up of the early warning radar chain, a revolutionary development chiefly due to Sir Robert Watson-Watt who evolved the apparatus, and Sir Henry Tizard, who recognised and guided its operational application.

Thus, the Royal Air Force prepared itself for what proved to be the only major, self contained and absolutely decisive air action in history, the Battle of Britain. The decisive feature of the battle was, however, that it prevented the defeat and occupation

The front line of Bomber Command 1939. *Above:* Blenheim. Below: Hampdens

Above: Whitley. *Below:* Early Wellingtons

of Britain and the Air Staff had never made the mistake of expecting more than that from it. Their hopes of contributing to the defeat of Germany had never been detached from Bomber Command and, despite the delay in its equipment and expansion which they had been compelled to accept in 1937, the Air Staff proceeded with the development of a series of bombing plans known as the Western Air Plans through which they hoped eventually to give expression to a strategic air offensive against Germany.

These plans included the possibility of attack on the German synthetic oil industry, her system of transportation, her sources of electricity and other forms of power, and they embraced too the idea of attacking the morale of the people directly. Other plans envisaged methods by which Bomber Command might contribute to the war at sea and on land by attacks on the German fleet and communications leading to the battlefield in France.

The Western Air Plans represented on the part of the Air Staff both an act of far-sighted faith and also one of perhaps unnecessarily blind faith. The plans were far-sighted in the sense that they provided for Bomber Command what was provided in no other air force in the world, a blueprint of remarkable strategic insight for a major bombing offensive. Many of the Western Plans were found in the later stages of the war to have not merely a general but even a detailed application to bomber forces in their stride. The plans also showed wisdom in the extent to which the somewhat exaggerated expectations of Trenchard were replaced by the more realistic view that Bomber Command would be one element in an offensive which would be naval and military as well; that, in other words, bombing alone would not win the war. Nevertheless, they showed courageous foresight in maintaining the belief even through Britain's weakest phase and darkest hours, that eventually she might find a formidable means of redressing her disadvantage through strategic bombing – as indeed she was to do.

But the Western Air Plans also had an element of blind faith in them. It is remarkable how the Air Staff allowed their judgement of bombing effect to be based upon a primitive multiplying of the factors in the Gotha attacks of 1917 and 1918 on London or the Luftwaffe over the Spanish towns during the civil war there. Even stranger was their failure to examine the problems of navigation and target finding which day bombing, let alone night bombing, would face in a long range offensive designed to take place by both day and night. Finally, it was unfortunate that the Air Staff failed to take cognisance, as far as Bomber Command was concerned, of the developments in air defence represented by what they themselves had introduced in Fighter Command, namely, very high performance all-metal monoplane interceptor fighters and the radar chain. This challenge to the use of the air by an enemy might surely have been expected sooner or later to apply to the heavy aircraft of Bomber Command. Yet the idea that bombing was a question either of self-defending formations in daylight or of evasion at night remained for Bomber Command tactically sacrosanct. Ultimately this proved to be the most serious defect in British air doctrine and it was one sufficiently mirrored in the United States to produce for them almost a calamity. For Germany, however, the consequence of neglecting almost entirely the possibilities of strategic bombing, produced for her in the end a very much more serious result. It is a remarkable fact that of all the belligerent powers of the Second World War, the only two which made systematic preparations for the sustained use of strategic bombing were Britain and the United States.

A Wellington crew : engines being run up

18

The opening of the offensive: September 1939– December 1942

At the outset of the war Anglo-French strategy was defensive. The Allies considered that time was on their side. It would allow them to build up and modernise their armed forces and thus to neutralise the advantage which the Germans had gained by preparing more effectively for war. In the meantime it would, so it seemed to the French and the British, be foolish to provoke German military action in the West. They were therefore glad to accept the relative inactivity of the so-called 'phoney war'.

Bomber Command fitted exactly into this general strategic conception. In September 1939, though thirty-three squadrons could be mobilised for war, ten were equipped with single-engined Battles and six with twin-engined light Blenheim bombers. Neither of these types had the range or lifting capacity to make a worthwhile contribution to the strategic air offensive against Germany and the Battles were in any case earmarked for the direct support of the British Army in the field in France. Thus there were in Bomber Command at the outset only seventeen squadrons which could be operational in the strategic air offensive. These were equipped with twin-engined Wellingtons, Whitleys and Hampdens, the heavy bombers of the period, but not, as the Air Staff well knew, the machines with which a major offensive could be made good. Hopes of that depended upon new machines, and especially the four-engined models, which had not yet come into operational service. Clearly then, there was wisdom in conserving the Bomber Command aircrews until they could be greatly reinforced in number and given better aircraft to fly.

Secondly, there was the consideration that it would be foolish to provoke the Germans into using their much larger air force in attacks upon Britain and France. Indeed, fear of a

knockout blow from the air had been a major preoccupation of the British and French in the last years of peace and it was certainly among the reasons explaining the difficulty which the British and French Governments had in standing up to Hitler. Now that they had done so, they saw no need prematurely to incur the worst consequences. This was another and more particular reason for holding back Bomber Command and for restricting such action as it was permitted to limited objectives.

This reasoning allied itself with another consideration – that of the moral issue involved in bombing which, like the weapon of naval blockade, was liable to involve entire nations and not merely their armed forces. Britain was reluctant to make the first move in a kind of warfare, namely strategic bombing, which was liable to arouse moral indignation and, in particular, she was anxious to retain the good opinion of the United States which she hoped would be a future ally. Indeed, on 1st September 1939, President Roosevelt appealed to the belligerents in the war which was then imminent to refrain from unrestricted air warfare.

There were, however, and in spite of these limitations, certain lines of action left open to Bomber Command which seemed to incur neither too much risk of excessive casualties nor of moral condemnation. These were, firstly, attacks of limited scale upon the German fleet, which none could deny was a legitimate military target and which, at least on occasions, could be attacked without undue risk of causing incidental civilian casualties and, secondly, long range flights of deep penetration to drop on the German people, not bombs, but propaganda leaflets. Not surprisingly, the attacks on German warships, which required little or no penetration of enemy territory and a high degree of bombing accuracy, were undertaken in daylight. The leaflet raids, which required long hours of flying

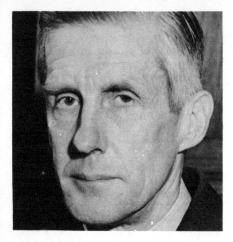

Sir Edgar Ludlow-Hewitt

Sir Charles Portal

over Germany and which did not depend for their effectiveness upon bombing accuracy were, also not surprisingly, attempted at night.

In the perspective of all that Bomber Command achieved and suffered in the war, these initial operations may seem of puny significance, but such would be a misleading impression. From Bomber Command's opening moves, though they did not involve strategic bombing, operational decisions followed which had a major and binding influence upon the course of the strategic air offensive which was to follow.

The Wellingtons of 3 Group failed to stand up to the German air defences in their attacks on German warships in September and December 1939. Twice, fifty per cent of the despatched force was destroyed and the loss in action of twenty Wellingtons from four operations on 4th September, 3rd December, 14th December and 18th December, 1939 was enough to establish in the minds of the British Air Staff that the heavy bomber could not in daylight survive in the face of the interceptor fighter.

At night, on the other hand, the leaflet bearing Whitleys of 4 Group ranged far and wide over Germany from the Ruhr to Hamburg, Berlin and Nuremburg and suffered battle casualties which were so light as, to quote the words used by the Group Commander in an official report, 'to lower in a surprising degree our opinion of the opposition we expected to meet'.

Since the hardships suffered by the Whitley crews from oxygen lack and intense cold clearly were remediable and since the leaflet raids gave no clue to and little hint of the difficulty of finding targets at night, the Air Staff decision to confine their major bombing operations, when they began, mainly to night actions seemed to be not only prudent, but more or less without penalty. There seemed no need to revise the strategic bombing plans which envisaged attacks upon specific targets such as oil plants or marshalling yards and no such revision was made.

Though German bombing in Poland at the beginning of the war was held by the British to have reduced the moral restraint which should be applied to their own air operations, Bomber Command was still held back from actions which might be regarded by enemies as provocative or by friends as outrageous. In the opening months of 1940, reconnaissance and leaflet raiding at night was the staple diet, not only of the 4 Group Whitleys, but now also of the 5 Group Hampdens and the 3 Group Wellingtons. The Luftwaffe too pursued a policy of wait and see but on the night of 16th March 1940 the Germans made a light attack on the Scapa Flow area. This was not strategic bombing since the targets were, of course, British warships and no important damage was done. All the same the Royal Air Force was not prepared to ignore this escalation of the war in the air, slight as it was. Three nights later, on 19th March, fifty aircraft of Bomber Command, thirty Whitleys and twenty Hampdens, were despatched with orders to bomb the German seaplane base at Hörnum on the island of Sylt during the night. Most of the crews believed they had located the target and hit it with the 500lb and 250lb high explosive bombs with which their aircraft were armed. Only one aircraft failed to return.

This was the first attack aimed by Bomber Command against a target on land. It was the portent of a vast offensive and it seemed to be a most encouraging beginning. On 8th April, however, photographic reconnaissance of Sylt was carried out. It showed no sign of damage to hangars and buildings at Hörnum or anywhere else. This was an indication that night bombing was going to be more difficult than expected and the Air Staff began to wonder about the success which their crews would have when the time came for them to begin a systematic offensive against inland German targets at night. Nevertheless, they could not return to the idea of heavy day bombing which, at least till more advanced aircraft came into service, had been destroyed by the German air defences.

The German attack on Denmark and Norway, which began on 9th April 1940, had given warning to the West of the speed, severity and skill of the German method which was about to knock France out of the war and bring Britain face to face with catastrophe. The Allied *débâcle* in Norway was not, however, enough to bring Bomber Command actively into the war. The British War Cabinet remained doubtful about the wisdom of initiating strategic bombing operations and the French, who thought they had all to lose and little to gain from that kind of war, were firmly opposed to an extension of it by Bomber Command. So, on 13th April 1940, Air Marshal Portal, who had just succeeded Sir Edgar Ludlow-Hewitt as Commander-in-Chief of Bomber Command, was told in his directive little more than that his forces should be held in readiness to meet various contingencies. It was, however, beginning to seem that the best objectives for a night offensive would be oil plants, which had a self-destructive element, railway marshalling yards, which had to use lights, and general harassing which might cause alarm, despondency and loss of sleep among the toiling masses.

At dawn on 10th May 1940, the German armies smashed their way across the neutral frontiers of Holland and Belgium and began the Battle of France. Five days later, the Dutch were overcome and the French lines were breached at Sedan. Rotterdam had been bombed by the Luftwaffe and the first major crisis of the Second World War was reached. On that day, 15th May 1940, the War Cabinet authorised Bomber Command to extend its operations from the battle-fields and their immediate lines of communication, to the heart of Germany. That night, ninety-nine aircraft of Bomber Command were despatched to attack oil and railway targets in the Ruhr. The strategic air offensive against Germany had begun.

The immediate requirement was to check the German advance towards Paris and the Channel Ports. The ulterior aim was to sap the strength of the German war machine by striking directly against the sources of its nourishment, such as oil production, the transport system and the war factories themselves. The immediate

Sir Richard Peirse

aim was pursued mainly in daylight and at a very high cost in casualties by the light bombers, the Battles and Blenheims, which, usually in the face of hopeless odds, sought the destruction of bridges and other immediate battlefield targets. There was, however, little that could be done in the face of overwhelming German superiority by these means and the inferiority of the French and British armies was rapidly exposed. Dunkirk was quickly followed by the capitulation of France on 17th June, 1940. This left only Britain between Hitler and victory in the war and it left Britain with only one remaining weapon capable of striking direct offensive blows against Germany. This weapon was Bomber Command.

Thus a premium was placed upon the ulterior aim of gradually undermining Germany from within by a strategic air offensive against her vitals. Not only did this appear to be a promising strategy. It appeared also to be the only alternative to yielding all initiative to the enemy and falling back entirely onto the defensive. The most hopeful line of action seemed to lie in Germany's oil industry. Oil was an absolute requisite of the war effort and modern mechanized warfare, in which armoured fighting vehicles and

aircraft played the key roles, demanded huge supplies of it. Without natural oil resources and denied her overseas lines of communication by British sea power, Germany was dependent to a high degree upon her synthetic oil production plants. It seemed that the German war effort could not long survive the dislocation of these plants, or the bulk of them, and this indeed was a perfectly correct conclusion, though it was later to be realised that Rumanian sources of natural oil played an important part in the overall German oil position.

In a directive of 4th June, the Commander-in-Chief had been told that oil targets would be Bomber Command's first selection. If they could not be found, aircraft factories would be the second choice. If neither could be found, then self-illuminating or otherwise identifiable targets would be bombed to bring about as great and as continuous a dislocation of German industry as possible. The instructions showed, and indeed specifically laid down, that targets had to be identified and aimed at. Indiscriminate bombing was forbidden.

Little progress had been made towards the realisation of these aims or, as experience was soon to show, towards the realisation that they could not be fulfilled, when Britain, owing to the collapse of France, became engulfed in what may well have been the greatest crisis in her history. This arose from the imminent threat of a German invasion and military occupation. It meant for Bomber Command that the immediate aim again thrust the ulterior strategy into the background. This time the immediate aim was principally the reduction of the scale of the offensive which could be mounted by the Luftwaffe against Britain and so, on 13th July 1940, Bomber Command was directed to afford top priority to the German aircraft industry. Oil targets, now at second priority, remained in the directive because the Luftwaffe, of course, depended on oil supply.

Coventry after the German attack in November 1940

Attacks were also to be continued against the yet more immediate targets offered by concentrations of invasion barges.

In truth, Bomber Command could not make much contribution to the Battle of Britain by direct action. As Sir Charles Portal pointed out to the Air Staff at the time, the German aircraft industry offered targets which were so small in size and at such great range from British bases that there was little or no hope of Bomber Command doing much damage to them. Yet Bomber Command unconciously did make a critical contribution to the British victory in the hour of her greatest peril. The Germans felt unable to attempt the invasion until they had secured an

effective command of the air over the English Channel and at least the southern part of England. The reasoning behind this decision was that while the British had air superiority in these areas they had the chance of bringing their greatly superior surface naval forces to bear upon the German lines of communication across the Channel and because, in the same circumstances, Bomber Command would be able to attack the German armies as they embarked, while they were in transit and while they disembarked. If however the Germans could gain air superiority then they could put the British

25

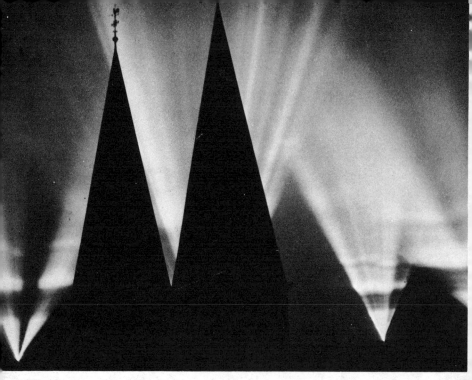

The German night defences

bombers and naval vessels alike to the sword. Thus it was the British fleet and Bomber Command which jointly drove the Germans to seek battle with the Royal Air Force Fighter Command. This, for Britain, was providential. Fighter Command was the sole element in the whole structure of the armed services of Britain which was not only ready for fully effective action but in all important respects was superior in tactics, situation and equipment to what the Germans had to offer. The result was a British victory as famous as Trafalgar and yet more decisive.

In the Battle of Britain, the Luftwaffe developed, by the standards of that period, a considerable bombing offensive against Britain. As the casualties by day became insupportable, the Germans, for the same reasons as the British before them and with more evidence to prove the case, turned more and more to night operations. This had the result that towns, rather than pin-point objects such as factories, tended to become the targets. On the night of 24th–25th August 1940 central London had its first taste of bombing since the Zeppelins and Gothas of 1916–1918. Early in September the main weight of the German attack was switched to night operations and London became the chief target. On the night of 7th–8th September bombs fell on the docks, Woolwich, East Ham, Poplar, Battersea, Bermondsey, Paddington, Bethnal Green, Waterloo Bridge, Westminster and Dagenham. The blitz had begun.

There was an immediate popular feeling, strongly represented by the Prime Minister himself, that the Germans should get as good as they were giving and indeed on the night of 25th–26th August, the night after the first German attack on central London, a force of Wellingtons and Hampdens of Bomber Command was despatched to attack industrial targets in Berlin. Pressure from Mr Churchill allied with the doubts about night precision bombing voiced by the Commander-in-Chief, Sir Charles Portal, tended in the direction of a more generalised assault on towns rather than upon specific targets in or near them and as more and more German bombs fell upon the residential areas of London and other British towns fewer and fewer scruples remained about where British bombs might fall.

Undoubtedly there was a considerable misunderstanding. Neither the British nor the Germans realised the very limited accuracy of night bombing. They did not yet appreciate that not only were the wrong areas in towns bombed but often enough the wrong towns were hit. The assumption with regard to each other's actions was that what was hit had been aimed at and so mutual recrimination and eventually mutual retaliation arose from the idea that, in both cases, the enemy was indulging in 'terror' bombing.

Nevertheless, the Air Staff continued to believe that selective bombing of particular targets was the best strategy and, to a considerable extent, they resisted the popular clamour and the advocacy of Mr Churchill. Despite a recommendation of 11th September 1940 from Sir Charles Portal that twenty German towns should be selected, warned and bombed, the Air Staff directed on 21st September that oil plants and railway targets were to be respectively the first and second priorities in the bombing offensive.

The Bomber Command crews who tried to carry out these idealistic directives in the summer and autumn of 1940 lacked even the means of gauging the extent to which they were impossible. Without any effective navigational aid they had to rely upon dead reckoning and good luck to bring them over their target areas. Without flares or marker bombs, they had to rely upon moonlight or instinct for the identification of their aiming points. Without cameras, they

Above: The remains of a Wellington down in Germany. *Below:* Air raid damage

brought back no more than fleeting impressions of what they had achieved.

The British bombing offensive, so far much less impressive than the German attack, was nevertheless getting under way. In September 1940, Bomber Command despatched 3,141 sorties in night raids. Sixty-five bombers failed to return and twenty-one more were destroyed in crashes after returning. The art of night fighting was as yet in its early infancy and, though the British bombers were occasionally picked up and destroyed by German night fighters, the principal hazards which they faced still came from flak, searchlight dazzle, icing and other weather dangers. There was also the risk, by no means slight, of getting lost and running out of fuel.

On 4th October 1940 Sir Charles Portal, who had been C-in-C Bomber Command since April, assumed yet greater responsibility as Chief of the Air Staff. His successor at Bomber Command was the former Vice-Chief of the Air Staff, Sir Richard Peirse. Thus, the advocacies of the Air Staff and of Bomber Command tended to be reversed. As C-in-C, Sir Charles Portal had been impressed by at least some of the difficulties of night precision bombing and had urged upon the Air Staff a more general policy of attack on German towns. Though not ruling this out the Air Staff had continued in the belief that night, selective attacks upon particular elements in the German war economy such as oil and communications would produce the better results. Now a different position arose. On 25th October 1940, the new C-in-C, Sir Richard Peirse, was sent a draft bombing directive which had Air Staff approval and which he was asked to consider. It showed that the Air Staff had two main aims in mind. The first was the destruction of German morale. The second was the destruction of German oil production.

The first aim was to be sought by selecting twenty or thirty German towns, choosing them carefully in the light of their size and the importance of the objectives which they contained and then attacking them repeatedly by forces of between fifty and a hundred bombers every few nights. When night visibility was reasonable and especially in moon periods, oil plants would be the main objectives. The Air Staff recognised that some effort would continue to be well used against marshalling yards and they knew that Bomber Command would have to contribute to the war at sea and in the air by occasional attacks on such targets as submarine yards and aerodromes.

Though the final directive, issued on 30th October, was somewhat watered down to meet Sir Richard Peirse's very reasonable objection that Bomber Command was being asked to undertake tasks well beyond the strength and accuracy which it possessed, the draft directive was truly the writing on the wall. It showed that the Air Staff, strongly supported by the Prime Minister and the Government, were now willing to acknowledge a policy of direct attack upon the German people in their cities as well as upon industrial and military installations in or near them. Nevertheless, these attacks were still designed to be the product of aiming at objectives within them. It was not till after the German attack on Coventry in November 1940 when the whole centre of the city, including its cathedral, had been ruined, that Bomber Command was instructed simply to aim at the centre of a city. This first such attack by the British took place on the night of 16th–17th December, 1940. The town chosen was Mannheim.

These developments, which were soon to become of so much greater importance when the impossibilities of the alternatives became more apparent, did not yet , however, adversely affect all of them and, in particular, the plan for the destruction of German synthetic oil plants now received strong reinforcement by an extraordinary piece of intelligence which was placed before the War Cabinet in December 1940. This suggested that Bomber Command had already reduced German production of synthetic oil by no less than fifteen per cent. This remarkable achievement, it seemed, had been brought about by a mere 539 tons of bombs which represented less than seven per cent of the total effort devoted by Bomber Command to industrial targets, communications, invasion ports and so on. This was the considered opinion of a special Cabinet Committee set up under the chairmanship of Mr Geoffrey Lloyd to advise upon the oil position of Germany and occupied Europe. Though the Lloyd Committee emphasised the importance of Rumanian supplies which, because of their distant range, were beyond the scope of Bomber Command, their reports also indicated the high degree of dependence which Germany had for high grade fuel upon her synthetic plants.

Though the estimates of the damage already done to German oil production by Bomber Command were presently shown to have been ludicrously optimistic, this was not apparent to the Air Staff at the time and it is therefore not surprising that oil was immediately given a higher pcsition in the bombing directive. Indeed on 15th January 1941, the C-in-C was told by the Air

Mannheim after the raid in December 1940

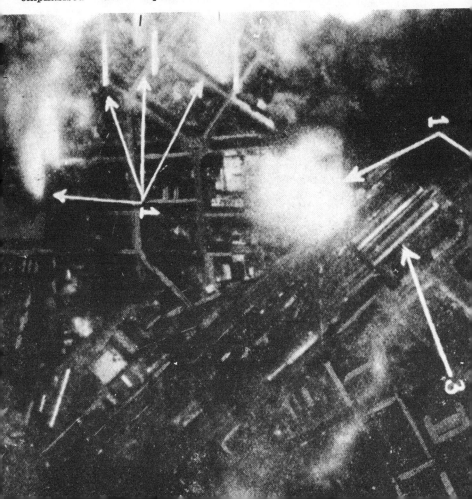

Lord Cherwell, Churchill's scientific advisor

Staff 'that the sole primary aim of your bomber offensive, until further orders, should be the destruction of the German synthetic oil plants'.

These really seemed to offer a most attractive target. The destruction of seventeen installations, which the Air Staff thought should be possible by the despatch of 3,400 sorties, would, it was believed, and rightly so, produce a catastrophic position for Germany. A further attraction was that nine of these plants were for a time thought to account for more than eighty per cent of the total production of all of them. What a chance, it seemed, to knock Germany out by a piece of minutely calculated bombing surgery.

The estimates of what Bomber Command had already achieved against oil targets as also those of what could be achieved by a greater concentration against them reckoned, of course, without the basic fact that, except for the occasional lucky chance, Bomber Command lacked the means of hitting such targets at night, whether in moonlight or not. In all the enthusiasm which was generated at the turn of the year for the oil plan in the Cabinet's intelligence committees and in the Air Staff, it seems that the Prime Minister was almost alone in sensing the real position. He was sceptical of cut and dried calculations. He doubted if the oil plan would lead to significant success. He regretted that oil plants were, for the most part, distant from populous centres.

The evidence was indeed already to hand, though for the time being no one seems to have noticed it. On Christmas Eve 1940, daylight photographic reconnaissance was carried out over the two synthetic oil plants at Gelsenkirchen. According to the records, these two plants had up to that time been attacked by 196 bomber sorties on which 262 tons of high explosive and an unspecified number of incendiary bombs had been dropped. It was seen that neither plant had suffered any major damage. As in the earlier case of the seaplane base at Hörnum on the island of Sylt, it was obvious that the bombs must have fallen somewhere other than on the targets.

The Air Staff were, however, saved by bad weather from what might otherwise have been a trial by exposure of their oil plan. In January, February and March, 1941, weather conditions restricted the oil offensive to a mere 221 sorties or only about half the number which had been flown in the last three months of 1940, before oil had the top priority. This compared with the 3,400 sorties which had been laid down as the number required to achieve the plan.

Before these matters could be given the consideration which they might otherwise have received, the bombing offensive was for the third time thrown out of gear by a major crisis of defence and survival. This time it was the Battle of the Atlantic. If the Germans through the use of their U-boats, their surface raiders and their long range Focke-Wulf Condor aircraft cut the British survival lines of communication across the Atlantic, Britain would starve and Germany would be victorious. If, on the other hand, Britain could frustrate the German offensive in the Battle of the Atlantic then she could survive but from that achievement Germany would not, of course, perish. This is why the Battle of the Atlantic was, from the British viewpoint, a defensive struggle, a struggle which had to be won to survive and develop other operations including the bombing offensive, but not a struggle in which Germany herself could be brought down or even reduced. So it was, if the war was ever to be won, that the effort devoted to the Battle of the Atlantic had to be rationed. In February 1941 Mr Churchill saw that the ration was not enough. On 9th March 1941 a new directive was issued to Bomber Command in which the Air Staff told Sir Richard Peirse of the need for him to give priority in the next four months to targets associated with the Battle of the Atlantic. Bomber Command, in short, was to be 'directed against submarine and long range aircraft activities whenever circumstances permit until the menace has been dealth with'.

Once again the development of the strategic air offensive and perhaps also the recognition of the operational limitations which beset it were impeded by the need for Bomber Command to shore up the national defences. All the same this by no means meant a complete change in bombing policy. If Bomber Command could not hit small industrial targets it was not likely to be able to hit small naval targets and, though this was an argument sometimes lost sight of by the advocates of direct participation in the Battle of the Atlantic by Bomber Command, it did often occur to the Air Staff and the C-in C Sir Richard Peirse was indeed soon to complain bitterly of having to throw some 750 tons of bombs into Brest Harbour in what he thought was the forlorn hope of destroying the *Hipper*, *Scharnhorst*, and *Gneisenau*. Such an effort would, he suggested, have been better spent on Bremen or Mannheim. As it was, a significant part of Bomber Command's reaction to the Battle of the Atlantic directive of March 1941 did consist of attacks on German towns with naval connections.

On 9th July 1941, without extending the four months period laid down for the Atlantic diversion by so much as a single day, a new directive was sent to Bomber Command. 'I am directed to inform you', the Deputy Chief of the Air Staff wrote to Sir Richard Peirse, 'that a comprehensive review of the enemy's present political, economic and military situation discloses that the weakest points in his armour lie in the morale of the civil population and in his inland transportation system'. The reasoning behind this gloss on the intelligence available

to the Air Staff was the operational conclusion that oil plants were too small to be hit but that marshalling yards would still be feasible targets on moonlight nights. For the remaining three-quarters of each month it was intended that the much larger targets offered by whole towns should be subjected to a heavy blitz or, as it was beginning to be called, 'area' bombing. The railway targets, mostly in and around the Ruhr, were selected with the aim of cutting off the rest of Germany and occupied Europe from this source of supply but they were also chosen because in most cases the aiming points lay near populous centres. The towns selected for area attack qualified, at least partly, because of their importance as railway centres. Thus, it was hoped that the two aims would be mutually supporting. Other towns: Hamburg, Bremen, Hanover, Frankfurt, Mannheim and Stuttgart, were added to the list to deny the Germans the opportunity to concentrate their fighter and flak defences.

While this very directive was being written, the operational evidence to show that the precision elements in it were still wholly unrealistic was coming to hand. That part of it which called for general area attack upon German industrial morale would require for its completion, as the Air Staff well knew, an enormously greater force than Bomber Command yet possessed. This expansion could only be achieved if the necessary

A Halifax comes in to land

production priorities were forthcoming and the area offensive could be undertaken with a chance of success only if that kind of attack remained the first priority in bombing policy. The irony was that the inaccuracy of night attack, which was more and more being revealed and which made the alternative of area bombing operationally more and more inevitable, also tended to reduce confidence in the idea of a strategic bombing offensive.

These seemingly counter-balancing factors were now, to a marked extent, to find their resolution in the relationship between a strategic circumstance which, at least to many, made it appear inconceivable that the strategic air offensive should be abandoned, and an operational investigation, which showed with unprecedented clarity that the only kind of major attack open to Bomber Command was area bombing.

On 22nd June 1941 the German invasion of Russia began. Whether or not Russia could withstand the onslaught soon became a burning issue. Britain, who had stood alone against Germany for a year, could but hope that Russia would survive and fight back. These new prospects did nothing to reduce the importance of the role of strategic bombing in Britain's grand strategy. On the contrary, they increased it. Britain could not bring military strength, or in significant degree, naval power to bear in support of Russia. It was simply impossible that in these circumstances she should abandon the bombing of Germany,

Lübeck, target for 28th March

the one means in her power of bringing immediate pressure to bear against Germany.

The British Chiefs of Staff were clear in their agreement upon continuing the strategic air offensive and upon the role which they foresaw for it. In a memorandum produced at the end of July they expressed their belief in the need to destroy the foundations of the German war machine: 'the economy which feeds it, the morale which sustains it, the supplies which nourish it and the hopes of victory which inspire it'. Only after that would it be possible to return to the continent and eventually to make a military contribution to the final defeat of Germany. 'It is in bombing, on a scale undreamt of in the last war', the Chiefs of Staff declared, 'that we find the new weapon on which we must principally depend for the destruction of German economic life and morale'.

Those who reckoned at the time, or the greater number who have since reckoned, that Britain might with advantage have abandoned her bombing offensive left, or now leave, out of account the basic grand strategic

conditions of the period. Without bombing there would not in Britain have been even the hope of eventual victory and without bombing there would not have been even the vestige of Russian gratitude which it, in fact, stimulated.

A further simplification of the issue was now at hand and the belief that there was still a major alternative to area bombing, even as small as that which had survived in the July Directive, was about to be annihilated.

The Prime Minister's Scientific Advisor, Lord Cherwell, sent a civilian investigator to Bomber Command in August 1941 to find out the answer to the increasingly raised question of how accurate or otherwise was night bombing. Though doubts had occasionally been expressed by the C-in-C, no systematic thought had been given to the question. Lord Cherwell's man now examined more than 600 photographs taken from night bombers during operations undertaken in June and July 1941. He also read the documentary records of these attacks. This research showed that of the aircraft which, on the basis of the written reports, were thought to have bombed their targets, only one third had, on

the basis of the photographic evidence, got within five miles of them. This was the overall conclusion. The evidence on which it was founded varied according to the geographical position of the targets, the weather conditions and the phase of the moon. Over the French ports results were much better than over the Ruhr and moonlight was shown to improve target finding capacity considerably. Perhaps the bleakest fact of all which emerged from the Butt Report, so called after its author, was that over the Ruhr only one-tenth of the bombers previously credited with having bombed their targets had in fact got within five miles of them.

Thus, it was shown, though as was stated in the report, on the basis of statistics which might in some cases be defective, that target areas were not 300, 600 or 1,000 yards around the aiming points. They were territories five miles around them. Two bombs within the target area might be up to ten miles apart. Moreover, it was shown that only a small proportion of the more successful bomber sorties were achieving even this degree of success.

The C-in-C and other senior officers in Bomber Command were at first inclined to look for the flaws in the Butt Report but not so Lord Cherwell. Neither for the first nor for the last time, he refused to delay his reaction while partisans and experts disputed the meaning of figures. 'However inaccurate the figures may be,' he told the Prime Minister, 'they are sufficiently striking to emphasise the supreme importance of improving our navigational methods.' Mr Churchill then made no bones about the report. He awaited proposals for action from the Chief of the Air Staff.

The real import of the switch from day to night bombing now became apparent. Drastic steps would have to be taken to improve the efficiency of Bomber Command but the prospect of precision attack at night was obviously an extremely remote and uncertain one. Nor was there any chance of returning to the idea of daylight attack. This had also been demonstrated in the summer of 1941.

When the Germans invaded Russia the need to draw air pressure off the Russians combined with the fact that so much German air power was now engaged in the east revived the idea of day bombing.

A series of attacks, known as 'Circus' operations, were carried out in daylight over France. The object was to bring the Luftwaffe to action. Targets were chosen within the strictly limited range of British fighters. They were attacked by Blenheims and sometimes by heavier aircraft, including occasionally the new four-engined Stirlings, so that the German fighters would be forced to intervene and thus to offer opportunities for the Spitfires which would arrive more or less in company with the bombers. The plan produced disappointing results basically because the Spitfires lacked the range to cross the German frontiers and the bombing was therefore in occupied territory about which the Germans cared less than their own. Their fighters therefore tended to intervene only when the tactical situation favoured them.

At the same time the theory of the self-defending day bomber was again tested using both the old Hampdens and the new four-engined Stirlings and Halifaxes. Attacks were made by small forces on Kiel, La Pallice and Brest. They achieved some success. For example, in the La Pallice attack at least five direct hits were scored on the *Scharnhorst* which sailed for Brest, as Captain Roskill has recorded in his history of *The War at Sea*, with 3,000 tons of flood water on board. The bomber casualties all the same proved to be unacceptably high. In the La Pallice operation, fourteen Halifaxes reached the target area. Five were shot down and the remainder were damaged by flak or fighter attacks. This was a fringe French target. Against targets in the interior of Germany it was once more made obvious that heavy bombers, whether modern or otherwise, could not be engaged on a regular war footing.

Sir Charles Portal's proposal then, to the Prime Minister, was that Bomber Command should concentrate in an offensive against German towns. If the attacks could be made as effective as the German operation against Coventry and if a sufficient number of German towns could be given that treatment then surely the aim of sapping Germany's internal strength would be accomplished. To do this Bomber Command would have to be vastly expanded in size. Its tactical methods would have to be thoroughly revised and scientific aids would have to be brought to bear upon its problems of navigation and bomb aiming.

Mr Churchill, with a touch of reluctance bred perhaps by earlier examples of Air Staff optimism, agreed. Bomber Command, which in November 1941 could marshal for operations no more than, on average, 506 aircraft, could not be suddenly expanded or improved. Yet what it most needed was some dramatic source of success to restore confidence in its future. But this too had to wait. On the night of 7th–8th November 1941, thirty-seven bombers from a force of 400 despatched to Berlin, Mannheim, the Ruhr and elsewhere, failed to return. These crippling losses were judged to be simply not worth the candle. Bomber Command had to live to fight another day, and especially so in view of the improvements and reinforcements which were now imminent. On 13th November 1941, the C-in-C was therefore told in a directive that the War Cabinet had decided that he should conserve his strength 'in order to build up a strong force to be available by the spring of next year'.

Thus, Bomber Command reached the nadir of its fortunes. The realisation of that fact was the making of the offensive both in the sense that it stimulated the radical development of bombing tactics and techniques and also in that it dictated the type of offensive which could be undertaken. The options had been exposed. The idea of area bombing was, in the main, the sole survivor. Specialist elements in Bomber Command and, as will duly appear, the air doctrine of the United States, were the exceptions.

During the last three weeks of 1941 and the first three of 1942 Bomber Command devoted more than a third of its entire effort to attacking the German battle-cruisers lying in Brest. Hopes of despatching the redoubtable vessels were not high and were not in fact realised. On 12th February 1942 the *Scharnhorst* and *Gneisenau* made their epic dash up the Channel and thence for home ports. This, as far as Bomber Command was concerned, solved the Brest question and opened the way for the resumption of a more vigorous strategic air offensive against Germany.

On 14th February 1942, a new bombing directive was issued. It laid down that the aim of the offensive would be focussed on the morale of the enemy civil population and, in particular, of the industrial workers. The primary targets were Essen, Duisberg, Düsseldorf and Cologne. These were all within range of the new navigational radar aid known as Gee which was now being installed in a proportion of the bombers. Other targets, including Berlin, which were beyond Gee range, were listed as suitable for attack if possible and some precision targets, oil, rubber and power plants, were included in case Gee proved accurate enough to make their destruction possible. To avoid confusion, the Chief of the Air Staff added a note to the directive pointing out that in the town attacks 'the aiming points are to be the built-up areas, *not*, for instance, the dockyards or aircraft factories ...'.

These instructions awaited the arrival of a new C-in-C. Sir Richard Peirse had taken his departure on 8th January. His successor assumed command on 22nd February. He was Air Marshal A T Harris. The new Commander-in-Chief inherited a force which in two years of war had failed to make any real dent in German strength, which had itself on many occasions been badly mauled and which was now at the centre of a controversy upon the outcome of which its future depended.

Russia had hung on and now it was the turn of the Germans to begin to suffer as they wintered on the approaches to Leningrad, Moscow and Stalingrad. In December, the Japanese attack on Pearl Harbor brought the United States into a fighting Grand Alliance. Not only were there now future potential methods of attacking Germany other than by bombing; there were also pressing crises of every kind from the Atlantic to the Middle East and from there to the Far East, where the Japanese swept all before them. Could Britain afford to go on investing in Bomber Command? Would its attacks ever become effective? Could not its aircraft be used for some more immediately useful purposes?

The Air Staff's belief in strategic bombing was assailed from all sides. The Navy wanted more and more squadrons for Coastal Command and it wanted new Coastal Commands in other theatres. The Government seemed to wobble and one of its most influential Ministers, Sir Stafford Cripps, who some believed would take over from Mr Churchill, told the House of Commons on 25th February 1942 that as far as Bomber Command was concerned a change of policy was on the cards.

On 30th March 1942 Lord Cherwell addressed a minute to the Prime Minister. In it he said that analysis of German attacks on Birmingham, Hull and other British towns had shown that 1 ton of bombs turned 100–200 people out of house and home. He reckoned that the average operational life of a Bomber Command aircraft was 14 sorties on which it could drop 40 tons of bombs and make between 4,000 and 8,000 people homeless. He discovered that in 1938 22,000,000 Germans lived in 58 towns each with a population of more than 100,000. He believed Bomber Command could find and hit these 58 towns. He expected that by the middle of 1943 Bomber Command would have

Scharnhorst (1) and *Gneisenau* (2) lying in dry dock at Brest, December 1941. The picture also shows an uncompleted dry dock (3) and a damaged oil tank (4)

received some 10,000 heavy aircraft. Half the bomb load of these would render a third of the entire German population homeless. Surely, Lord Cherwell suggested, that would break the spirit of the people.

As was quickly pointed out, the statistics and perhaps the science of this argument were somewhat open to question. Nevertheless, Lord Cherwell's minute had a simplicity, a clarity and a decisiveness which redressed the strategic debate in Bomber Command's favour and afforded Air Marshal Harris a chance to show what could be done.

On the night of 28th March 1942, 234 aircraft of Bomber Command set course for the mediaeval, half timber constructed city of Lübeck on the Baltic. For the first time the new navigational aid Gee, new bombing tactics, a new bomb load proportion and some of the new bombers were tried in action at the same time. Lübeck was beyond Gee range, but the crews which had the device on board had a much improved chance of finding the target because they could keep to the right track on a good part of the outward journey and so reduce their dependence upon dead reckoning and good luck. The Gee equipped aircraft, some flown by specially selected crews, were therefore placed in the van and ordered to illuminate the target with flares and, as far as possible, to set it on fire with incendiaries. This was intended to make it

conspicuous to the main force following up with, for the most part, less experienced crews and without Gee. Most of these too carried maximum incendiary loads. Thus, the idea of communicating the benefits of the greater skill of some crews and the advantage of Gee, still in short supply, to the whole force was put into practice. Thus too the idea of exploiting the self-destructive capacity of the target, that is its inflammability, instead of trying to knock it down piece by piece was put to the test.

The result was an extraordinary success. 191 of the returning crews claimed that their attacks had been delivered in the target area. The subsequent investigation of the photographic evidence, now a highly sophisticated art, fully confirmed this encouraging indication. Then, photo-graphic reconnaissance, carried out in daylight on 12th April, showed that nearly half of the entire city, amounting to some 200 acres, had been devastated. It looked as though 2,000 houses had been destroyed or ruined. Several factories, the electricity generating station, some warehouses and the railway station had been destroyed or damaged; so had the Reichsbank, the Market Hall and the Cathedral. For the first time in the war a Bomber Command attack on a German town caused concern not only in the town itself but also some panic in Berlin where normally events on the Russian front were of much greater interest than any Bomber Command activity. Bomber Command had served notice of a scourge which might yet consume the Germans who then were beginning to reap the

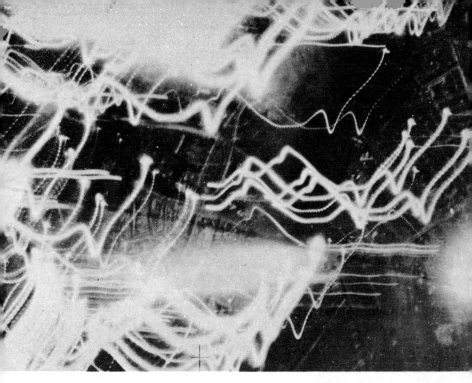

Above: Long exposure photograph during the Lübeck raid. *Below:* The damage

harvest of what they had sown. Much of the tactical conception of the Lübeck attack was inspired by German methods over England in the preceding winter.

Lübeck, however, had only a slight relevance to the main strategic plan for Bomber Command. It was not a town of major industrial importance and it was chosen more because of its suitability for an operational experiment than on account of its strategic significance. The main prizes, as the February directive had signified, lay in and around the Ruhr, farther to the west, within Gee range, but also inland, heavily defended and often obscured by industrial haze. And of all these, the one with the most magnetic attraction, because the Krupps works lay at its centre, was Essen.

Here and hereabouts Bomber Command, try as it would, could not recreate the success it had achieved at Lübeck or even the lesser but still impressive results of the attacks soon after on Rostock. Inland targets were, of course, more difficult to find than coastal ones because, at night, if anything natural at all was visible, the difference between sea and land was the easiest thing to recognise. There were also other difficulties protecting the Ruhr and the various targets to which the Germans attached the greatest importance. If the bomber crews flew below 10,000 feet, they were liable to be blinded by searchlights and flak and they also became highly vulnerable to the latter. If they flew above 10,000, and preferably above 15,000 feet, these difficulties and this hazard were considerably reduced, but from that altitude there was virtually no chance of being able to identify and aim visually at the right target area. Successful area bombing, depending as it did upon a concentration of attack around a given aiming point or series of aiming points, could not be achieved by inaccurate bombing. Gee proved to be not accurate enough as a blind bombing device and therefore the target area still had to

be seen to be hit: initially actually seen and subsequently seen from the fires burning in it and the flares dropping on it. This had been possible at Lübeck. The attacks were made from fairly low altitudes, and for that reason were expensive in casualties, and the operation took place on a moonlit night with the full assistance of a coastline on the spot. Essen was a different order of problem.

Another difficulty was the rapidly increasing effect of the German night fighter force. At the beginning of 1942 about one per cent of Bomber Command's sorties were destroyed by night fighters. By the summer this percentage had risen to more than three-and-a-half. In the period from August – October 1941 3·2 per cent of Bomber Command's night sorties failed to return and 1·4 per cent of the returning crews reported that they had been fired on by night fighters. In the same period of 1942 the missing rate was 5·3 per cent and the survivors attacked rate was 2·9 per cent. A missing rate of five per cent over a sustained period of about three months was the maximum which Bomber Command could afford if it was to survive as an effective fighting force. Since this is not a fact which can necessarily be immediately grasped and since it is also of fundamental importance to the understanding of the strategic air offensive, it requires a brief explanation.

To the missing rate, that is the crews who failed to return from operations to England, there had to be added the loss of those crews who had been injured and those who were injured or killed in crashes after returning or on non-operational test flights and those who became ill or collapsed. If from all these causes, seven per cent of the Bomber Command sorties resulted in the loss of the crews, and if during this time each crew was embarking upon a tour of thirty operations, then, of every hundred crews starting a tour, ninety would be lost. Apart from the possible

Lieutenant-General HH Arnold

Squadron Leader J D Nettleton VC

effects upon morale of such slender survival chances, there was the more immediate consideration of what would happen to Bomber Command when it reached the point that nearly every crew was on its first attack. The meaning of this was that whenever the Bomber Command missing rate seemed to be sticking at or above five per cent discretion had to intervene to modify valour.

Radar, now just beginning to come to the aid of the bombers in the dark, was indeed a double edged weapon for it was also coming to the aid of the German night fighters and anti-aircraft gunners. Bomber Command was therefore confronted more and more with the problem not simply of how to keep the German defences spread but also of how to confuse and swamp them.

One method of attempting the latter course was to increase the size and concentration of the attacks. As the German night fighters were organised and directed within zones and each fighter operated in a 'box', it seemed likely that the same number of bombers passing through the 'box' would be shot down regardless of the number entering it and there was thus the basis of the hope that, by stepping up the concentration, the

percentage of losses would be reduced. The same consideration, for slightly different reasons, was likely to apply to radar laid anti-aircraft guns. There was too another reason for wanting to increase concentration and also the size of the attacks. This was because, by the greater chance offered that the German fire-fighting and re e services would be swamped, there arose the hope of a much increased destructive dividend per ton of bombs dropped.

For these reasons Bomber Command set its sights upon much larger forces, upon passing those forces across Germany in much closer company and upon carrying out the bombing at the target within a much shorter time than, for example, at Lübeck where the attack had been planned to last for more than an hour-and-a-half. Night bombers, without navigation lights and except for fleeting glimpses, were invisible to one another and apart from slip stream buffets from time to time hundreds of bombers could cross Germany in virtual ignorance of each other except when they caught fire or collided. The tactics of concentration therefore turned upon accurate navigation which now became a subject taken very seriously in

Bomber Command. New and remarkable aids were on the way to reinforce Gee. The second pilot in Bomber Command was abolished. Specialised bomb aimers took the vacant place and allowed the old observers to become specialised navigators. Thus the four-engined heavies carried a pilot, flight engineer, bomb aimer, navigator, wireless operator, mid upper gunner and rear gunner.

The tactic of bombing concentration turned upon clearer target indication. One method was to pick the most experienced crews to indicate the aiming point with flares as at Lübeck. Another was to create a specialised element specifically trained and equipped for the purpose. After much argument about the merits and dangers of a 'corps d'élite' the second course was chosen and in August 1942, the Pathfinder Force came into being. It was to be manned by specially chosen crews and given the best and the latest equipment.

The whole essence of the tactic of concentrated and massive attack lay however in numbers. On this score Bomber Command, throughout 1942, remained very weak. In November 1941 there had been available for operations each night an average 506 aircraft with crews. In May 1942 this number was 417 and in January 1943 it was only 515. It may therefore be thought remarkable that at five minutes past noon on 30th May 1942 Sir Arthur Harris gave the order 'Thousand Plan Cologne'. That night 1,046 bombers set forth from England to bomb Cologne in what was at that time the greatest air operation in the history of warfare. To do this, the C-in-C had committed his entire front line strength and he had marshalled every available aircraft and crew, some with rather slender and others with slightly archaic experience, from the operational training units of Bomber Command. It was a translation of theory into practice before the real substance had been created. It was to be a preview of what could

be done with an enlarged Bomber Command. It was an amazing risk and it produced a memorable success.

At five o'clock the next morning a Mosquito pilot on reconnaissance looked down from 23,500 feet upon a pall of smoke rising to 15,000 feet in the shape of a cumulo-nimbus cloud. 600 acres of Cologne had been devasted. Forty British bombers had failed to return and another 116 had come back damaged. At last Bomber Command had scored a major success against a major target. Despite the failure of two further 1,000 attacks against Essen and Bremen, and despite an autumn and winter of disappointing and often costly operations, Bomber Command was now well and truly on the map and in the allied grand strategy of the war.

The American Air Staff, under the leadership of General H H Arnold, was not so well impressed by these achievements as the British Air Staff, the C-in-C and, indeed, the Prime Minister would have wished. Since the United States Eighth Air Force was, throughout 1942, working up and building up on English bases in preparation for an intervention in the strategic air offensive against Germany, this was of more than academic interest.

The Americans were determined to mount their offensive in daylight and they intended it to be a precision attack upon key points in the German war economy. In fact their theory of strategic bombing was in many respects similar to that with which the British had entered the war. The surprising thing was that the British experience of bombing in action, which had led them to abandon major daylight operations and then, because of the conditions at night, to adopt the tactics of area attack on large targets, had left the American idea unscathed. There were various reasons for this. The Americans undoubtedly were determined that their contribution to the offensive should be a distinctively American effort. Though the United States made a vast contribution to Bomber Command, for example, by the production of Packard built Merlin engines for installation in Lancasters, there was no question of the Eighth Air Force being added to Bomber Command as a reinforcement. Like General Pershing's Army in the First World War it was to be a separate American manned and American commanded element in the military alliance. Secondly, the Americans had evolved, developed and were now on the point of introducing operationally a remarkable and, for its period very advanced, four-engined long range bomber, the B17 Flying Fortress. An early version had been tried by Bomber Command and found most unsuitable for night bombing owing, among other reasons, to very prominent exhaust flames. The newer versions being sent to England carried much more formidable armament than the British heavy bombers, they were capable of flying at very high altitude and for these reasons looked promising for daylight flying. Thirdly, the initial American bomber crews were highly trained in the difficult art of close formation flying and hardly skilled at all in that of navigation. Fourthly, much American bombing doctrine came from trials in Texas where the visibility from great heights is often very good. Finally, the Americans had been impressed by the inconsequential effects of British night bombing in Germany during 1940 and 1941 when, as a neutral country, they still had diplomatic and business contacts there.

The British Chief of the Air Staff, Sir Charles Portal, was greatly perturbed. He foresaw, and as bitter events were to show rightly so, that the American idea of heavy bombers operating in daylight and depending for their survival upon their own defences, would end in disaster. He did his best to persuade the Americans to convert to night bombing, but he soon saw that the Americans had

hung their hats on the daylight idea and that if he continued to oppose their plan, the only result would be an American withdrawal from the strategic air offensive against Germany.

The issue between Bomber Command and the Eighth Air Force, between Portal and Arnold and even on occasion between Churchill and Roosevelt, was not between accurate and inaccurate bombing. They all wanted accurate bombing. Nor was it even between general bombing, in the sense of simply striking hard at identifiable targets whatever they might be, and selective bombing, in the sense of concentrating upon some particular and vital element in the enemy system and trying to dislocate it. The issue was simply between day and night bombing; between what, on the British side,

B17 Flying Fortresses and their escorting fighters weave a pattern of vapour trails

seemed to be the possible and the impossible and what, on the American side, seemed to be the worthwhile and the worthless. The irony is that despite the wisdom, the foresight and the courage which pervaded both camps, neither perceived what, as events were later to make clear, was the main issue. The double irony is that neither the British nor the American idea could have succeeded had either surrendered to the other.

These prospects which were to be unveiled through grim experience into triumphant outcomes were, however, alas for the British and the American bomber forces, in the still distant future. In 1942 the only notable incursion into Germany in daylight was British. On 17th April 1942 Squadron Leader J D Nettleton led a formation of twelve Lancasters of 5 Group in a low level attack upon the MAN works at Augsburg where U-boat engines were made. Of the twelve crews who set out, only five returned and Squadron Leader Nettleton, so far from establishing a tactic of war, was awarded the Victoria Cross. In 1942 American day bombing was of a different kind. The attacks were delivered from high level in formation where the bombers could afford each other mutually supporting defensive fire. It was also confined to German occupied territory outside Germany, in which the German air defences still had a strictly limited interest. It began at Rouen on 17th August 1942 when twelve bombers of the Eighth Air Force attacked the marshalling yards there without loss.

The combined bomber offensive: January 1943 - March 1944

In January 1943, Churchill and Roosevelt met at Casablanca in North Africa with their military advisors to discuss the future conduct of the war. The Germans and Italians had been swept out of Africa, Italy would shortly be invaded by way of Sicily and eventually the main invasion of Europe would be undertaken across the Channel and by way of Northern France. As far as bombing was concerned there were two problems. Firstly, there was the question of what was expected of it and therefore of what order of priority it should be given. Secondly, there was the question of how the British and American contributions might be adjusted one to the other so as to generate a combined bomber offensive.

A great deal has been written about this famous Conference at Casablanca and those who attended it must indeed have believed that they were participants in, or at least observers of, great historical developments. It may, however, be doubted if this was really so. The great strategic *dénouements* of the war proceeded much more from the generation and demonstration of operational capacities than from discussions between Churchill and Roosevelt or even between their chiefs of staff. Now that military invasions of the continent were becoming possibilities, it more or less followed that the object of strategic bombing should be to prepare the way for them by weakening the enemy's heart. There was therefore nothing specially notable in the Casablanca formula which laid down that the primary object of bombing 'will be the progressive destruction and dislocation of the German military, industrial and economic system, and the undermining of the morale of the German people to a point where their capacity for armed resistance is fatally weakened'.

This, nevertheless, did indicate the role which bombing was to play. It made it clear that it was not expected to win the war on its own, but that it was meant to produce a situation in which victory could be won by the armies. Such was the Casablanca solution of the problem concerning the role of bombing in relation to the Allied war effort as a whole. It did not, of course, affect Sir Arthur Harris's hope that his area bombing would all the same be sufficient of itself to bring about the collapse of Germany. Nor did it settle the question of how Bomber Command's operations and those of the American Eighth Air Force might be combined. In practice, the Casablanca directive, which listed most of the objectives of bombing,

Lancasters in formation

Above: **Bomber version of the wooden Mosquito.** *Right:* **The Lockheed Ventura light bomber**

almost regardless of whether they were feasible or not, left Bomber Command and the Eighth Air Force to follow their own methods as best they could.

In 1942, indeed, Bomber Command had demonstrated not only the ability to develop a night area bombing offensive but a relative inability to develop anything else. For that reason the main lines of Bomber Command's operational policy in 1943 were virtually decided before the Casablanca discussions. The prospect for the area offensive in 1943 was now, however, radically improved by a number of developments of the first importance to Bomber Command. Both the quantity and the quality of the front line were on the verge of a leap forward. The number of aircraft available with crews for operations had, for more than fifteen months, stuck at or below an average of about 500. It now, at last, began to increase significantly and by March 1944, despite tremendous casualties, it reached an average of 974. During 1942 the most obsolete and the worst aircraft in Bomber Command were phased out of the operational squadrons. Thus, the Blenheims,

which had never been up to their role, the Hampdens and the Whitleys which had been overtaken by old age and the Manchesters which had failed were consigned to lighter duties or, in the last case, to the scrap heap. This left the Lancasters, Halifaxes, Stirlings, Mosquitoes and Wellingtons in possession together with a few Venturas, Bostons and Mitchells, imported from America to fill the place of the Blenheims. Though the Halifaxes and Stirlings were beginning to appear as considerable disappointments, the Lancaster was peerless as a heavy bomber and the Mosquito, as a light bomber which could carry a 4,000lb bomb as far as Berlin, was also in a class of its own.

Science was now in addition coming rapidly and effectively to the aid of the crews who flew these machines. For most of 1942, the only radar aid available had been Gee. But on 20th December 1942 a new device, known as Oboe, came into operational service. On the night of 16th January 1943 the Pathfinder Force dropped its first target indicator bombs on operations and, on the night of 30th January 1943, H_2S received its operational baptism.

Oboe enabled aircraft to follow radar beams to their targets and to achieve considerable accuracy in locating them blindly up to, approximately, the range of the Ruhr. The device could only be used by a few aircraft at one time and the range was proportionate to the altitude of the bomber. Oboe was thus an excellent aid to target marking by Mosquitoes of the Pathfinder Force which could reach much greater altitudes than the heavy Lancasters. But the value of Oboe could not have been communicated by a few Mosquitoes to the many heavies without the ingenious and conspicuous target indicator bombs, which were now supplied to the PFF. The third device, known as H_2S, gave the navigator a radar map of the ground over which he was flying and was thus an important aid to navigation and target location. While, however, the contrast between land and water usually showed up well, the map produced in other circumstances was often extremely difficult to read.

It was true, on the other side of the coin, that the German air defences and especially the radar directed night fighter force, had also made great forward strides but Bomber Command was hoping to contain that situation by a combination of larger numbers of more concentrated bombers to swamp the defences and the introduction of radio countermeasures.

These improvements and these challenges would soon be put to the test in the Battle of the Ruhr which began in March. In the meantime Bomber Command was once again called into the Battle of the Atlantic at naval insistence and, much against the wishes of Sir Arthur Harris, it had to direct no fewer than 3,170 sorties against Lorient and St Nazaire, French towns which were principal U-boat bases. Alas, as Bomber Command had expected, practically everything was destroyed except the U-boat pens which had

Above: Bostons show their lines
Right: Mitchells queue for take-off

56

heavy concrete cases. There was also a little offensive against Italian targets, to meet the Prime Minister's view that the time had come to turn the heat on there. For the rest, Germany received a curtain-raiser for what was to come including an attack on Berlin, the first since November 1941.

The Americans, whose ideas of daylight selective bombing had received so much of the limelight at the Casablanca Conference, were still not able to do much. In January 1943 they still could not muster as many as a hundred bombers for an attack.

The Avro Manchester

Since they were going to depend over Germany upon mutual support in tactical formation for their defence, they reckoned that such a force was not large enough to undertake anything very ambitious. For this reason it was fortunate that emphasis was placed in the Casablanca directive upon U-boat targets since at least their bases were on the coast and did not involve penetration of enemy territory.

Though American efforts in the first half of 1943 could thus at best be described as little more than tentative and experimental, 27th January 1943 was nevertheless an historic date. It marked the first attack by the Eighth

Air Force on Germany. Its Commander, General Ira Eaker, despatched ninety-one bombers to attack U-boat targets at Wilhelmshaven. Fifty-three of them were credited with carrying out their orders, two attacked U-boat targets in Emden and three were lost. Thus, the B17 Flying Fortresses and B24 Liberators received their baptism of fire over Germany beyond the range of escorting fighters. Thus too the Germans saw the beginning of another development in the air war which after many curious and bitter crises was to bring them to ruin.

The directive of February 1942 had pointed to the Ruhr, and within the Ruhr, to Essen as a prime target for Bomber Command in the pursuit of its area bombing offensive against the heart of German war industry and the morale of German industrial workers. Throughout 1942, the Ruhr in general and Essen in particular had, however, with the heavy searchlight, anti-aircraft gun defences and the protection of a lingering industrial haze, proved to be beyond the destructive capacity of Bomber Command. All this was to be changed in the Battle of the Ruhr which began on the night of 5th March 1943 when Harris despatched a force of 442 bombers to Essen. As usual the target area was shrouded in a thick smoke haze and it is probable that but for one new factor, it would once again have escaped the brunt of the attack. The new factor consisted of eight Oboe equipped Mosquitoes from 106 Squadron.

The crews of these eight Mosquitoes had orders, operating entirely on Oboe indications, to drop salvoes of red target indicator bombs on the Krupps works at intervals from the zero hour, which was set for 2100 until thirty-three minutes later. These initial markings were then to be sighted by the crews of twenty-two heavy bombers of the PFF, who were ordered to back them up by aiming green target indicators at them. The main bombing force would then

attack, aiming at the red and green markers, and compressing its blow into the forty minutes immediately following the zero hour. The bomb loads were to be two-thirds incendiary and one-third high explosive. The success of the attack therefore depended upon the accuracy of the initial blind marking by the Oboe Mosquitoes, the visibility of the target indicators through the haze and cloud and the necessary degree of navigational accuracy to bring sufficient of the markers and bombers to the right place at the right time. Such was the plan.

The battle began two minutes early at 2058 when an Oboe aimed red target indicator went down on Essen. It immediately attracted a shower of bombs from the main bombing force which was also a minute or so early in arriving. Five minutes later the green backing-up markers began to cluster around the original red. A clear, and as later became apparent, an accurate aiming point in the centre of Essen was established and well maintained until at 2138 the last green backers-up went down. Three of the Mosquitoes failed to turn up owing to technical failures and one dropped its marker two-and-a-half miles wide of the aiming point owing to a failure in its Oboe equipment. Fortunately for the success of the operation this error came later in the proceedings and many of the bombing crews diagnosed it correctly. Fortunately also some of the bombers turned up a couple of minutes early. Otherwise the initial red marker might have failed to focus the attack as effectively as it did.

When the returning aircraft had yielded their photographs and these had been analysed by the Operational Research Section of Bomber Command, it appeared probable that 153 crews had dropped their bombs within three miles of the Krupps works. Over such a difficult target as Essen this was a completely unprecedented success. Daylight photographic reconnaissance carried out on 7th and 8th March brought striking confirmation. The photographs showed exceptionally severe damage. The very centre of the town was devastated. 160 acres had been laid waste and in other areas, amounting to 450 acres, three-quarters of the buildings had been destroyed or damaged by fire and explosion. The Krupps works themselves had been heavily damaged. This was the first of five major attacks on Essen to

H₂S signals transmitted from the aircraft were received back in various intensities depending upon the nature of ground beneath the aircraft. The result is indicated by the photograph of an H₂S display (right) and an actual map of the same area (left)

which, during the Battle of the Ruhr, some 2,070 sorties were despatched. Heavy attacks were also made on Duisburg, Düsseldorf, Dortmund and Bochum in the Ruhr. In all these operations the technique of Oboe marking was used and in many of them heavy devastation was caused. Goebbels, who was responsible for morale, and Speer, who was responsible for war production, began to express serious concern and special labour battalions were transferred from working on the Atlantic wall-defences to undertake repairs in the Ruhr.

The Battle of the Ruhr was, however, by no means confined to the Ruhr towns. Bomber Command had to keep the German air defences spread out

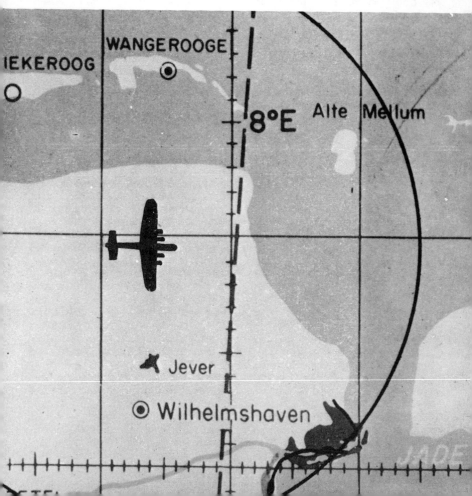

and there were great numbers of very important area targets all over Germany. While therefore the Ruhr itself was the hub of operations during the campaign from March to July which became famous as the Battle of the Ruhr, there were other attacks on targets as widely separated as Berlin, Stettin, Pilsen, Munich, Stuttgart and Nuremberg. The scale of these operations was also extremely varied and ranged in fact from the effort of a single Mosquito, sent on the night of 21st June to bomb Hamborn, to the force of 826 bombers despatched on the night of 23rd May to Dortmund. The small Mosquito attacks carried out by anything from 1-13 aircraft were designed to cause a nuisance and to mislead the Germans as to where the main attacks would fall. Of these main attacks, there were in the Battle of the Ruhr period some 43. They involved the despatch of 18,506 sorties. 872 aircraft failed to return and another 2,126 were damaged or came to grief after recrossing the English coast. Thus, somewhat more than 16 per cent of the aircraft sent out in major actions of the Battle of the Ruhr became casualties of one sort or another and 4·7 per cent of them disappeared.

Bomber Command surmounted these losses in two senses. The morale of the force was high and the average number of aircraft with crews available for operations had increased from 593 when the Battle began to 787 immediately after it ended. While,

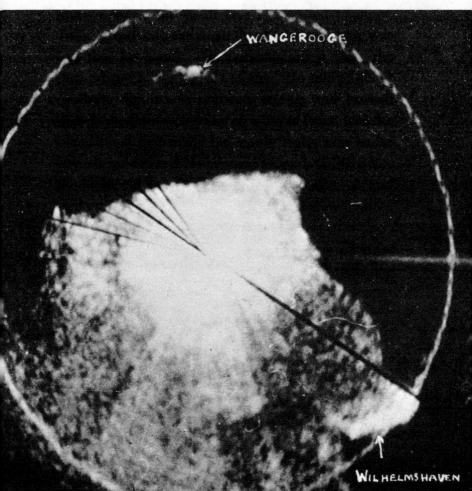

however, the Mosquitoes, flying sometimes at 30,000 feet or more, showed themselves to be virtually immune to the German night defences, there was disquieting evidence of further improvement in German night fighter tactics which were now assisted by Bomber Command's radar transmissions and also its target and route marker bombs.

Nor was the reward for Bomber Command's sacrifices by any means always as rich as that reaped over the Ruhr when the attacks were within the range of Oboe. In the attacks farther afield, such as that for example against Nuremberg on the night of 8th March 1943, different marking tactics had to be used. On these occasions indeed H_2S was often put to a severer test than it was able to meet. In the Nuremberg operation, on which 335 aircraft were despatched, the plan was for an advance force of five H_2S equipped bombers to drop illuminating flares in the target area three minutes before zero hour, relying entirely on their H_2S indications. The crews would then, it was hoped, identify the aiming point visually in the light of the flares and aim green target indicators at it. Two minutes later this process was to be repeated by nine more H_2S equipped bombers, all of course, from the Pathfinder Force. Thus, it was hoped to establish a clear and central aiming point for the main attack. In all cases the PFF crews were told to launch their target indicators blindly, on H_2S indications only if the flares failed to make visual aiming possible.

Of the fourteen initial illuminating and marker crews, six arrived in the target area with their H_2S out of order, some made visual identifications of what they thought was the aiming point. Others aimed their markers by H_2S. Two were shot down. The result was a somewhat scattered series of markers and the absence of a clear central aiming point. Though considerable damage was done to Nuremberg, the bombing lacked the concentration which had been achieved at Essen. H_2S, despite the advantage of its unlimited range, had nothing like the accuracy of Oboe, and though H_2S marking techniques were occasionally very effective it was only occasionally that Oboe techniques were ineffective.

The aim of all these area attacks was to achieve the greatest possible concentration of bombing in an area of not more than three miles around the aiming point. In this way it was intended that uncontrollable fires might be started and irreparable damage done to the city centres. Much depended upon accurate time-keeping and upon accuracy in the dropping of the initial markers. This was difficult enough, even within Oboe range, though it might be and often was achieved to a sufficient degree for the purpose in mind. Bomber Command had, however, never relinquished the hope of achieving much more precise results than these.

While Sir Arthur Harris persevered with the general area bombing offensive which he had been instructed to undertake, experts of various kinds and classes proliferated in the Ministry of Economic Warfare and other mushroom war-time bureaucratic growths. These were responsible for an underlying suspicion that area bombing was rather a crude and indirect method of prosecuting the war and that there must somewhere be a clever dodge by which the problem of defeating Germany could be short-circuited. Sometimes the Air Staff were not only seduced by such theories but were guilty of adding conviction to them. Thus there was a school of thought which suggested that the downfall of Germany would be brought about by the destruction of two ball-bearing plants in Schweinfurt. Thus, too, a belief had grown up that the destruction of the Ruhr dams would produce decisive results.

From this febrile theory there sprang what was the most gallant and the most celebrated achievement of

0 Miles 100
0 Kilometres 150

BALTIC SEA

NORTH SEA

Kiel
Rostock
Stettin

NETHERLANDS

Elbe

Berlin

Oberhausen
Münster
Essen Gelsenkirchen
Dortmund
Duisburg Bochum
Krefeld THE RUHR
Wuppertal
Mülheim
Düsseldorf
Aachen
BELG Cologne

Weser

G E R M A N Y

Rhine

Frankfurt

CZECHO-
SLOVAKIA

Pilsen

LUX

Mannheim

Main

Nuremberg

FRANCE

Stuttgart

Danube

Munich

AUSTRIA

SWITZERLAND

Sorties despatched to targets

between 1000-2000 ⊙ between 500-1000 ● less than 500 (Major operations)

Bomber Command in the Second World War, the breaching of the Möhne and Eder Dams, and a result which, though unforeseen, was none the less important for that reason. From the breaching of the dams there came for Germany a disaster from which she recovered almost immediately. But for Bomber Command there came the origin of a technique of bombing which, when later transferred to target marking, was to revolutionise the capacity of the force.

Since before the war thought had been given to possible schemes for the destruction of the Ruhr dams. Now, in 1943, the possibility of such an achievement seemed to exist. Dr Barnes Wallis had designed a fantastic rotating bomb, which, if correctly delivered, would skip across the water in a series of diminishing bounds like a flat stone cast with a wristy throw upon a smooth water surface, and would then, as a spent force, come to rest against the dam wall, sink to the bottom and there detonate and so shake the structure at its base. This design, which might be used against a dam or a ship – the *Tirpitz* was the candidate – had, by the middle of February 1943, caused what Harris described as 'all sorts of enthusiasts and panacea mongers' to career around the ministries with schemes for modifying a suitable number of Lancasters to carry the bomb.

To this Harris was strongly opposed. He thought the bomb would not work

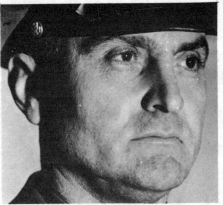

Left: **B17 Flying Fortresses**
Above: **General Ira Eaker**
Below: **Wing Commander Guy Gibson VC**

and he also thought that low-level operations involving heavy bombers would be 'costly failures'. Here indeed was the rub. The Wallis bomb when it was built showed an obstinate tendency not to bounce but to break up when it hit the water. In the end, it seemed that all would be well if it could be dropped from a height of not more than sixty feet, and if this was done so accurately that exactly the right number of skips were executed before it reached the dam wall. If it was dropped too soon, it would sink out of contact and be wasted; if too late, it would strike the structure too hard, detonate on the surface and blow up, not the dam, but the bomber. Despite these daunting prospects, (no one, for example, knew how a Lancaster could be flown at exactly sixty feet; it certainly could not be done by eye or by altimetre) Portal thought the experiment must be tried. Three Lancasters were earmarked for modification. Then it was decided to attempt the dams, especially the Möhne, Eder and Sorpe. Twenty-one bomber crews with special operational experience were formed into 617 Squadron in 5 Group and placed under the command of an officer, already famous in Bomber Command and soon to become a hero, Wing Commander Guy Gibson. Under the most hush-hush conditions this band of gallant and resourceful men rehearsed and rehearsed again the dambusting tactics which were soon to confer an undying fame upon their squadron.

Step by step the problems were overcome until, on 15th May, Wing Commander Gibson briefed his crews for their endeavour. The approach to the Ruhr was to be at night in moonlight, at a low level, never more than 1,500 feet, in the hope of keeping under the German radar. One wave of nine Lancasters, operating under Gibson's immediate command would attack first the Möhne Dam then the Eder and finally, if any bombs were then left,

Left: Window. *Below:* Devastation in the Ruhr

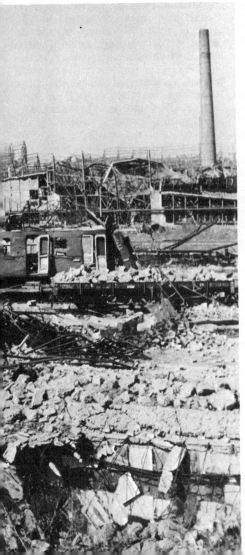

the Sorpe. The second wave of five aircraft was to attack the Sorpe and the third wave, also of five aircraft, was to act as a mobile reserve which would get its orders from 5 Group HQ during the action. Communication between aircraft and 5 Group HQ was to be by morse code carried by W/T (Wireless Telegraphy). Communication between the aircraft on the spot, and therefore the means of Wing Commander Gibson actually commanding his force, was to be in plain English by VHF R/T (Very High Frequency Radio Telephone).

Just before half past nine on 16th May 1943, 617 Squadron began to take off from its base at Scampton. Of the first wave one was shot down on the way out. Gibson successfully marshalled the other eight over the Möhne lake. He then settled his Lancaster at sixty feet, focussing two spotlights on the water beneath as the means of measuring the height and flew straight at the dam through a hail of cannon fire. His bomb fell and seemed to skip correctly but the dam did not breach. The second Lancaster, flown by Flight Lieutenant J V Hopgood went in. It was hit, burst into flames, dropped its bomb late and was blown up. The third Lancaster flown by Flight Lieutenant H B Martin went in. Though Gibson came too to divide the fire, Martin's Lancaster was hit and badly damaged. Its bomb fell about twenty yards short. Then came the fourth Lancaster, flown by Squadron Leader H M Young and, despite the damage to his aircraft, in came Martin with him to draw off the fire. Young's attack looked perfect, but again the dam did not breach. The fifth aircraft, flown by Flight Lieutenant D J H Maltby was called in and for the third time the attack looked perfect. But when the spray subsided, the dam was still there. Gibson was calling for the sixth attack when suddenly the dam collapsed and released a flood. Gibson marshalled the three Lancasters which still had bombs and Young's, since he was the deputy leader, and set course for the Eder dam. Here there was no flak but nearby hills made it difficult to manoeuvre. Flight Lieutenant D J Shannon made several unsuccessful attempts to gain the correct altitude and direction of approach and Gibson then called in Squadron Leader H E Maudsley's aircraft. Its bombs fell fractionally late and blew up the Lancaster. Shannon then tried again and this time executed a perfect attack. The dam remained and Pilot Officer L G Knight approached with the last bomb. It fell, bounced, struck and sank. The dam gave way and a second flood was released. In a flash the news was transmitted to 5 Group HQ and thence to Washington where an allied conference was in progress. A glorious and spectacular feat of arms had been achieved. Perhaps nothing of quite comparable skill and daring had ever before or has ever since been achieved from the air. Wing Commander Gibson survived to receive the VC, to fight and to die another day. The attacks on the other dams failed and the damage caused by the breaching of the Möhne and Eder dams was quickly contained by the Germans. The cost to 617 Squadron was terrible. Eight Lancasters failed to return and two more were so badly damaged that they had to abandon the operation. Thus, in a single operation, nearly half the Squadron was lost.

Harris's scepticism of everything, save the functioning of the bomb, was proved by events to have been justified and had he now decided to disband the Squadron, his decision would scarcely have caused surprise let alone criticism. Some inspiration, however, caused the C-in-C to brush aside the difficulties of recruiting replacement crews of sufficient calibre. He determined to keep 617 Squadron and despite further crippling losses in September 1943 when an unsuccessful attempt to breach the banks of the Dortmund-Ems canal resulted in the survival of only three

of the eight Lancasters despatched, it survived. In time the accuracy of its dambusting technique availed not only to destroy targets of special importance and difficulty but more important to place markers as guides to the massive destructive power of Bomber Command as a whole.

From the Dams Raid there thus came the means of reintroducing the possibility of precision bombing at night, not just for a few specialised crews, but for all Bomber Command. This prospect however still lay a considerable way in the future. In the meantime Bomber Command had to grapple with the more immediate difficulty of making general area bombing more generally accurate.

After the major destructive raids which characterised the Battle of the Ruhr and the astonishing achievement of 617 Squadron in breaching the Möhne and Eder dams, the prestige of Bomber Command and its Commander-in-Chief reached a new high level. Now, with a force of growing strength and increasing versatility, the campaign of area bombing was to be further developed towards the culminating point. Harris saw reason, from the terrific devastation in many German cities which was already achieved and from what he shortly intended to add to it, to hope that Germany would topple and collapse from these effects alone. Portal did not share this expectation. He thought that the invasion of Europe by Anglo-American armies would have to be carried out and that it would be no picnic but a hard fighting advance. He did believe, however, that the bombing could play a vital role in sapping German strength and thus making the invasion at least possible and perhaps, relative to what it might have been, more certain of success. If the German leaders, and especially Goebbels and Speer who were among the most concerned with maintaining the home front and its contribution to the German war effort, had had to judge between these two expectations they would already have been hard put to it to decide. After the opening phase of the Battle of Hamburg, they would have veered sharply in favour of Harris's view.

At the end of July and the beginning of August 1943, on the nights of 24th, 27th and 29th July and 2nd August to be precise, Harris despatched 3,095 aircraft in 4 major attacks on Hamburg. Some 9,000 tons of bombs, about half of them incendiaries, were cast into this assault and the result was the most comprehensive and catastrophic devastation and slaughter yet caused from the air. Hamburg suffered in 4 nights what all Britain suffered from German air raids in the entire war. About 50,000 Germans were killed and nearly another 40,000 injured. Upwards of 1,000,000 fled the stricken city. More than half the houses or flats in Hamburg were destroyed and about half the factories were destroyed too. When he realised what had happened, Speer exclaimed that 6 more attacks like that would finish the war. Yet in achieving this colossal result, Bomber Command had suffered much lighter casualties than usual. From the 3,095 sorties despatched, the German air defences had claimed only 86 aircraft or 2.8 per cent. Though another 174 bombers had been damaged, the total casualty rate was only 8.4 per cent as compared with, for example, the 19.9 per cent which had been suffered by the 2,070 sorties despatched to Essen in the 5 attacks made on that city during the Battle of the Ruhr.

Nonetheless, the 6 comparable attacks, which Speer had apprehended, did not take place and indeed it was not until the Bomber Command attack on Dresden in February 1945, that Germany was again to suffer a comparable disaster. Hamburg, though of course not entirely, recovered. Speer regained his confidence. The German war effort weathered the storm without serious inroads upon its production, or amazingly enough, its morale. The reasons for the success of Bomber Command over Hamburg were particular and they could not be repeated in the campaign which followed on the road to Berlin, nor, as bitter events were to show, in the Battle of Berlin itself.

The reason for the extraordinary degree and scale of destruction in Hamburg was the unprecedented concentration of the bombing in time and space and this, in turn, was due to the exceptionally accurate marking of the target and the also exceptionally accurate navigation of the main bombing forces which resulted in the great majority of the aircraft, except on one night when the weather was very bad, arriving at the right time and the right place. In their turn, these achievements were due, in part, to the exceptionally clear indications given on the H2S radar screens carried in all the marking aircraft and many of the bombing ones and, in part, to the unusually ineffective performance of the German night fighters, flak and searchlights.

The specially good H2S performance was due to the special position and characteristics of Hamburg. The contrasts between land and water and between built up and open country happened to show up with unusual clarity. Probably no other important city in Germany gave such a good H2S picture on the, by later standards, comparatively crude sets which were then available to Bomber Command. The failure of the German air defences either to exact their usual toll or to harass the aircraft during their bombing runs was due to the confusion caused to the radar system by the introduction of 'window' by Bomber Command.

Window consisted of metallised strips of paper cut to the appropriate wavelength and then dumped in large quantities at intervals from the bombers. This produced radar responses in swamping quantities. The blips on the German screens which represented the British bombers and by which the German controllers and

Sorties despatched to targets

between 2000-3000   between 1000-2000   less than 1000   (Major operations)

Battle of Hamburg 24th July – 18th November 1943

fighter observers had previously directed many of their night fighters and laid much of their flak were now lost in a mass of window responses. This measure took the Germans by surprise and though they adapted their tactics so as to overcome at least some of the protection which window afforded the bombers, these developments did not come in time to rescue Hamburg.

The phase of the Bomber Command campaign, conveniently described as the Battle of Hamburg and the approach to Berlin, which was initiated on the night of 24th July 1943 with the first of the four great attacks on Hamburg, was, however, by no means so favoured as at its very outset over Hamburg itself. In this phase, which lasted until 18th November, when the Battle of Berlin began, there were thirty-three major attacks on German cities including Bochum, Essen, Düsseldorf and Remscheid in the Ruhr, Hanover, to which like Hamburg more than 3,000 sorties were despatched, Bremen, Kassel, Frankfurt, Mannheim and Stuttgart in the central complex and Munich, Nuremberg, Leipzig and Berlin, to which more than 1,000 sorties were sent, in the east. There was also a specially orientated attack on Peenemünde where, it had been discovered, the Germans were testing and developing V weapons – the forerunners of missile warfare which were to cast an anxious shadow over Allied victories in the last year of the war.

In addition to these major attacks on German cities, Bomber Command also operated in force against Milan, Turin and Genoa in Italy as well as against various special objectives in France. Moreover, on operations carried out independently of the heavy bombers, small forces of Mosquitoes were out on 75 nights harassing the Germans everywhere from the Ruhr to Berlin and back again and without much loss to themselves. Indeed from the 819 Mosquito sorties involved only 13 failed to return. By comparison, the major operations, carried out principally by Lancasters, Halifaxes, Stirlings and Wellingtons, were much more expensive. In fact from the thirty-three major attacks on German targets which involved the despatch of 17,021 sorties, some 695 bombers failed to return and another 1,123 were damaged, some to the extent of being complete losses. Even so, the missing rate of 4·1 per cent and the total casualty rate of 10·7 per cent bore favourable comparison with the Battle of the Ruhr in which the corresponding figures had been 4·7 per cent and 16·2 per cent.

This encouraging reduction in the casualty rate which enabled Bomber Command to maintain its offensive and to increase its rate of expansion was undoubtedly due in considerable measure to the introduction of window and it underlined the folly which had been committed by delaying the introduction of this countermeasure for more than a year after it became available on the ground that its use by the Germans would disrupt the British air defences. Mr Herbert Morrison, the Home Secretary of the period, who was a particularly obstinate advocate of this precaution, seemed unconvinced by the fact that the Germans hardly had a bombing force to be fended off and that the disruption of air defence was therefore likely to favour the British much more than the Germans. But of course Mr Morrison was responsible for the home front and could not perhaps be expected to take a more than parochial view. Nor, unfortunately, was he the only offender in this respect.

There was, however, another important reason for the reduction in Bomber Command's casualties. The geographical concentration of its attacks was less intense than in the Battle of the Ruhr and particularly in the second half of it. This undoubtedly confronted the Germans with a

greater problem of defence. Surely though, the most disappointing aspect for Bomber Command was the failure to repeat or even to approach the awesome successes which were achieved over Hamburg in the opening phase. Clearly Bomber Command had not yet found the way to ensure the establishment of a plain and accurate aiming point and the necessary degree of navigational accuracy to exploit it to the full as a generality, especially when beyond the range of Mosquitoes fitted with Oboe which was still limited to about the distance of the Ruhr. Moreover, the speed of the recovery of the German night fighter force from the window set-back gave cause for some concern. The Germans could still easily detect the general direction of the main bomber stream and by a system of 'running commentary' they found the means with increasing success of directing their night fighter pilots into it. There they had tremendous opportunities for picking up targets which relative to themselves travelled slowly, could evade but sluggishly and belched conspicuous flame from their exhausts. Even so, Hamburg was by no means the whole of Bomber Command's success. Many other German cities had to bear a lesser but still terrible ordeal and Bomber Command performed many brilliant feats.

Among the greatest of these was the attack on Peenemünde on the night of 17th August 1943. Three specific aiming points were allotted to the force of 597 heavy bombers despatched, since the object was to destroy particular buildings connected with the rocket research activities rather than as usual to cause general havoc to the housing, communications,

Left: The Möhne dam breached by 617 Squadron. Bombers left a 200 foot gap in the dam, and flooded the ground below it. *Above right:* American incendiary bombs fall on U-Boat yards in Hamburg

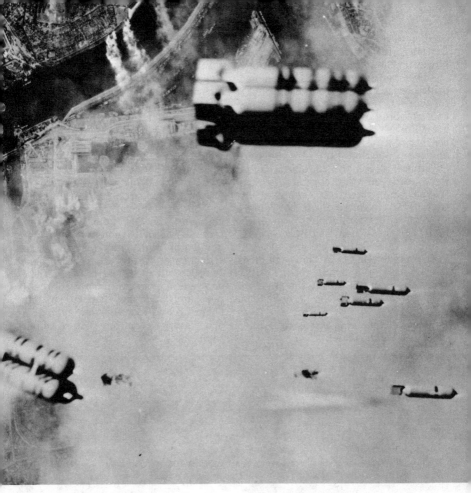

municipal facilities and so on. The force, for the first time in a massive operation, was controlled over the target by a master bomber as Wing Commander Gibson had controlled 617 Squadron over the dams. The officer chosen was Group Captain J H Searby, who commanded 83 (PFF) Squadron. His persistence in remaining in the most hazardous conditions over the target throughout the attack and in directing it over his radio telephone made an important contribution to its accuracy; so did a new form of marker bomb consisting of a 250lb case packed with impregnated cotton wool which was designed to burst and ignite at 3,000 feet and then to burn vividly on the ground for as long as ten minutes. These formidable and conspicuous markers, soon to become famous in Bomber Command as 'Red Spot Fires', were hard for the Germans to put out or to simulate and, if only they could be put in the right places, had a great potential for focussing area attacks on the selected areas.

The conditions of visibility, including bright moonlight, which were required to achieve the order of accuracy needed in the Peenemünde operation as well as the long duration of the flight to reach the research station, made the target a particularly dangerous one. From the attack forty of the bombers failed to return and thirty-two more were damaged. The destruction caused was considerable and an optimistic interpretation of the effects on German V weapon development was made by the British intelligence experts. In fact, however, these effects were much less than hoped. Even so, it seemed probable that the introduction of the V2 was delayed by up to two months, though some of this effect may have been due to other bombing attacks on the other sites. V1 development was scarcely affected at all. Several buildings in which V2 experiments were going on were completely destroyed and about 700 workers at various levels up to Professor Thiel, an expert on propulsion, and Herr Walther, the Chief Engineer of the project, were killed in the attack. Peenemünde was yet further evidence, though this was by no means fully appreciated in Britain at the time, of the truly formidable proposition

which Bomber Command was up against. The Germans showed amazing resourcefulness in redeploying their Peenemünde development programme elsewhere and getting on with it. The expectation of this was among the reasons which led Harris to doubt the wisdom of bombing aimed at selective purposes. He thought the Germans would find a way round the sort of difficulties which might be caused by selectively taking out a ball bearings factory, a research station or a dam and he was indeed generally proved right by the Germans in this. The trouble was that, though the Germans could not really get round the destruction of whole cities, and hence Harris's wish to destroy them, they showed an extraordinary resourcefulness and stoic heroism in patching them up and carrying on, even when the damage was on the Hamburg scale.

Peenemünde showing extensive damage after the attack

The alternatives of selective and general aims, the alternative between choosing a particular element in the German war economy and concentrating upon it, and that of causing the greatest and the widest possible general dislocation, was now, however, a burning issue not so much because of Bomber Command's experience but because of what had happened to the American Eighth Air Force. To see this, we must now, therefore, turn back from November 1943 when the Battle of Berlin was about to begin to March 1943 when the Americans had begun to intensify their daylight assault on Germany.

By April 1943, General Eaker considered that his daylight bombers had proved their ability to penetrate the German air defences and carry out a precision bombing campaign against key elements in the German war economy represented by the industries producing submarines, aircraft, ball-bearings, oil, synthetic rubber and military vehicles. Success, he claimed, was a question of the expansion of the force and he asked for 944 Fortresses and Liberators to be in the United Kingdom by July 1943, 1,192 by October 1943, 1,746 by January 1944 and 2,702 by April 1944 when the final phase of the offensive was due to begin.

Certainly, the need to expand American heavy bomber strength based in England was obvious and urgent if the Eighth Air Force was to get effectively into the bombing offensive against Germany. Though, in April 1943, there was an average daily heavy bomber strength of 337, only an average of 153 were fully operational and American bombing raids therefore continued to be restricted to a very small scale by comparison with the regular British effort. The depth of American penetration also continued to be limited to the fringes represented by targets in France, other German occupied territories and the coastal areas of Germany herself such as Emden, Wilhelmshaven, Vegesack, Bremen, Flensburg and Kiel.

Eaker's claim to have proved his ability to penetrate in daylight rested therefore on tenuous experience. All the same Portal, who had been charged at Casablanca with the direction of the combined bomber offensive, supported it and the Americans began to pour the required reinforcements of aircraft, men and materials across the Atlantic. The difficulty and the danger was that neither the Americans nor the British had any high performance fighters with the range to reach the areas in which the American bombers would have to bomb. The American bombers could not, in daylight, hope to avoid the German fighters, nor, of course, could they outpace them. Their only hope therefore seemed to be to stick together in their formations and hope their guns would keep the Germans off. They could also seek to bomb aircraft production and its components, such as ball bearings, at a high priority so as to reduce the German supply of fighter aircraft. They could also hope that the British Bomber Command would help them by making area attacks on cities specially connected with fighter aircraft production or its components, such as, for example, Schweinfurt, the centre of the German ball bearing industry.

These were the factors which led in June to the bombing directive, known as the Pointblank directive, placing special emphasis upon the need to attack the German aircraft industry and its component production, especially those parts concerned with fighter production. 'It is emphasised,' the directive said, 'that the reduction of the German fighter force is of primary importance; any delay in its prosecution will make the task progressively more difficult.'

This last consideration had particular force. German fighter strength was increasing and the more it did so, the less good were the bombing, especially the day bombing, prospects. Secondly, the German aircraft

Doctor Barnes Wallis

Albert Speer

industry was dispersing and the more it did so, the more difficult it would be to find really profitable targets in it. Already, the German aircraft industry was an especially difficult and dangerous objective. Many of its most important factories lay at extreme range in the eastern half of Germany and the factories themselves were often subdivided into small units which were hard to hit.

In this situation, the American day bombers, which in reaching quite short range targets were already suffering alarmingly high casualties, were confronted with a particularly unenviable task. To make their operations safer they had to attempt attacks which were much more dangerous. On 17th August 1943, Eaker despatched his greatest attack yet consisting of 376 Fortresses and ordered them to undertake by far their deepest penetration. The targets were the ball bearing plants at Schweinfurt and the fighter aircraft production factory at Regensburg. The American bombers, 315 of which were credited with having delivered their attacks in which they dropped a total of 724 short tons of bombs were heavily engaged by the German air defences. Twenty-four Fortresses of the Schweinfurt wave and thirty-six

of the Regensburg wave were shot down. Thus, sixteen per cent of the despatched force was lost. This was more than three times the casualty rate which could be afforded in a sustained offensive. It gave an indication, for the first time in realistic terms, of what the prospects of a daylight heavy bomber offensive were when the targets lay in the interior of Germany. Eaker could do little else than pull his horns in and there were no more deep penetrations of Germany by his bombers until October.

By that time, the German air defences had grown yet stronger. According to British intelligence estimates, the Luftwaffe had by 1st October some 800 single-engined and 725 twin-engined fighters defending the western air approaches, and these estimates were not far out. In fact, on that date the Germans had for this purpose, 964 single-engined and 682 twin-engined fighters. This was nearly 400 more than when the Pointblank directive had stepped up the emphasis placed on the importance of reducing the German air defences. The Pointblank directive, in fact, as all concerned began now to recognise, simply was not working out as far as the American day offensive was concerned. Despite their losses and despite the

Group Captain J H Searby

damage they had done at Schweinfurt, Regensburg and elsewhere, the Luftwaffe was losing neither strength no effectiveness, at least on the western front.

In this desperate situation, American eyes turned back to Schweinfurt, the home of the German ball bearing production. The destruction of the plants there would, they believed, deal German aircraft production a crippling blow and, for the second time they resolved to make the attempt. 291 B17 Flying Fortresses were despatched to Schweinfurt on 14th October 1943. The formations were divided into two forces of roughly equal strength which proceeded on their way with a thirty mile gap between them. Groups of P47 Thunderbolt fighters of the Eighth Air Force were ordered to accompany the bombers up to the limit of their range which, despite the addition of special drop fuel tanks, could not yet carry them beyond the area of Aachen. This was a long way short of Schweinfurt. Other P47s were ordered to meet the bombers as they returned and escort them on the last sixty miles or so of their homeward journey. Royal Air Force Spitfires were also to carry out sweeps during the final stages of the withdrawal. These plans were an indication of the extent to which confidence in the idea of the 'self-defending' bomber formation, so high at the beginning of the year, had already collapsed. The execution of the operation completed the process.

The Germans forebore to engage in force until the Americans reached Aachen and parted company with their P47 escorts. Then they closed in and the Fortresses came under attack from wave after wave of German fighters firing machine-guns, cannon and rockets. Though crippled long before they reached it, the American formations pressed on to Schweinfurt where it seems 228 Fortresses succeeded in dropping 395 short tons of high explosive and 88 short tons of incendiaries on or near the ball bearing plants which suffered considerable damage. Then the bombers turned for home. 60 of them did not make it and another 138 got back damaged, some beyond repair. The appalling fact was that from the original force of 291 bombers, 198 had been lost or damaged. This was the worst disaster in the history of air power which had yet befallen a major bomber force and the Americans simply could not carry on their offensive. It is perhaps scarcely surprising that they grossly exaggerated the number of German fighters which they had shot down on 14th October, inflating what was probably between 30-40 to 186, and they also enormously overstated the strategic effect of the bombing. General Arnold, the Commanding General of the United States Army Air Forces, even lent authoritative credence to the view that it would not again be necessary to bomb Schweinfurt, so complete had been the destruction of the factories.

This was, however, at best wishful thinking and, despite the severe problems which the attack caused them, the Germans found the means of solving their ball bearing crisis. They had, in fact, already given much thought to the problem in advance. Speer now appointed Philip Kessler as

special commissioner for ball bearings. Enquiry showed that stocks were better than had been expected, ingenuity showed means of reducing the number of ball bearings required and also the number of different types which had to be produced. Arrangements with Sweden made it possible to increase imports of the types most urgently needed. Considerable dispersal of future production was executed. By these and other means, Speer's staff, and especially Kessler, largely neutralised the effects of 14th October.

Harris, who had long since been pressed to bomb Schweinfurt, had always opposed the idea largely on the grounds of what had now happened. But though he had anticipated the extent to which the Germans would be able to recover from the bombing of Schweinfurt as also the extent to which allied intelligence experts would have exaggerated the dependence upon this particular selective or as he called it 'panacea' target, Harris's view was not agreeable to the Air Staff and to Portal, the Chief of it, in particular. Mounting pressure was now put on Bomber Command to launch a major area assault on Schweinfurt. Thus the British were called upon to pull the American chestnuts out of the fire, or so it seemed.

In truth, the issue was more complicated than that. The need to deal with German air superiority in the battle over her territory arose not only from the requirements of the American daylight bomber formations. It was concerned too with the impending invasion of Normandy by the Anglo-American armies which was due to take place in May 1944.

Harris believed he could clinch the situation by carrying the night area

Two of Hitler's secret weapons, the V1 (far left) and V2 (left). These so-called 'vengeance' weapons were Hitler's answer to the bombing of Europe

bombing offensive to its climax in the Battle of Berlin. If the Americans would also come in on it, he told the Prime Minister, in November 1943 Berlin could be wrecked from end to end. 'It will cost between us 400-500 aircraft. It will cost Germany the war.' Portal too hoped the Battle of Berlin would advance the allied cause but he did not believe it could produce such a decisive consequence as that. He believed that Bomber Command must contribute to the reduction of German air strength, vital to American day bombing and the Normandy invasion alike, by bombing Schweinfurt and other towns associated with fighter production. Such tasks he accepted as necessary diversions from the general area offensive and the attacks on Berlin itself. Meanwhile the Americans, forced back into relative inactivity in the bombing offensive, had turned their attention to the introduction of long range fighters, to the introduction, in fact, of machines with Spitfire-like performance and the equivalent of B17 Flying Fortress range. Before the end of the Battle of Berlin, now on the point of being launched by Bomber Command, the consequences of this new American preoccupation were to show themselves in decisive form.

On the night of 18th November 1943 Sir Arthur Harris despatched 444 aircraft of Bomber Command to Berlin. Only 9 of them failed to return. Such was the promising first shot in the greatest bombing assault upon a single target which, up to that time, had been known. It was followed between then and the night of 24th March 1944 by 15 further major Bomber Command attacks on Berlin. These operations involved the despatch of 9,111 sorties, 7,256 of which were flown by Lancasters, 1,643 by Halifaxes, 162 by Mosquitoes and 50 by Stirlings.

Britain replies to the V1 threat with heavy attacks on the installations in northern France

From them, 492 bombers failed to return, 95 were destroyed in crashes after regaining the English coast and another 859 got home damaged. In addition to these 16 major attacks, there were also 16 minor harassing actions against Berlin which involved the despatch of 186 Mosquito and 22 Lancaster sorties. As the Battle neared its end a development which could scarcely have been anticipated at the time of the Schweinfurt operation in October 1943 occurred. The Americans joined in. Their first attack on 4th March resulted in only a few of their bombers getting to Berlin but, in the second on 6th March, more than 600 did so. On 8th March nearly 500 American bombers arrived over Berlin, and on 22nd March the Eighth Air Force despatched another attack more than 600 strong.

This unprecedented and predominantly British assault on Berlin certainly achieved in its proportions what Harris had told the Prime Minister would be required to wreck it from end to end. At the end of March 1944, however, Berlin, though very severely damaged, had not been wrecked from end to end. 400-500 bombers had been lost but it had not, as Harris had expected, cost Germany the war. On the contrary she continued to fight on the eastern front against the Russians, in Italy against the British and the Americans and she was to offer stiff resistance to the main Allied invasion in France and then on her own territory for nearly a year after the initial landing in Normandy. Her war production continued to rise until July 1944 and though that was the month of the famous but ineffective plot against Hitler the bulk of the nation stood behind him in a fight to the last.

Bomber Command, on the other hand, emerged from the Battle of Berlin so badly mauled that a change of both strategic direction and tactical method was forced upon it. The engagement which had been joined on the night of 18th November 1943 not

only was, but had to be, broken off after the attack on Nuremberg on that of 30th March 1944. Thus it seemed that all the tactical development, increase in power and concentration of effort which had been built up after the rebuff of November 1941, which also centred on Berlin, had travelled full-circle and come to nought.

From the Nuremberg operation on the night of 30th March, on which 795 aircraft were despatched, 94 failed to return, 12 were totally destroyed after returning and another 59 were damaged. This was a missing rate of 11·8 per cent and a total casualty rate of 20·8 per cent. If not quite as bad, in terms of proportions, as what had happened to the Americans at Schweinfurt, this outcome in its full context produced an equally important effect. It represented, as the Schweinfurt operation had done, a major victory for the German air defences.

The full context of the Nuremberg operation was, of course, the Battle of Berlin, which in the same sense as the Battles of the Ruhr and of Hamburg, is taken to embrace not only the hub of the actions but all the major attacks which Bomber Command carried out against Germany in that phase of its operations. In this sense, the Battle of Berlin consisted not just of the sixteen major attacks on Berlin but also of nineteen major attacks upon Ludwigshafen, Leverkusen, Frankfurt (four attacks), Stuttgart (four attacks), Leipzig (two attacks), Stettin, Brunswick, Magdeburg, Schweinfurt, Augsburg, Essen and Nuremberg. All these operations took place between 18th November 1943 and 31st March 1944. In total, they involved the despatch of 20,224 sorties. 1,047 bombers failed to return and another 1,682, including several beyond repair, were damaged. Yet at no time during the Battle of Berlin did the front line of Bomber Command, as represented by the average number of aircraft available for operations during a given month, reach 1,000. In fact, in November 1943 this average was 864 and in March 1944 it was 974. Thus, more than the equivalent of the front line during the Battle of Berlin was left on the ground in Germany or at the bottom of the sea.

Several of the attacks caused massive damage. Field-Marshal Milch, Chief of Aircraft production, told his staff in February 1944 that Berlin could not endure such an ordeal indefinitely. He feared that when the big cities had gone then it would be the turn of the smaller ones and, indeed, the path of devastation which Bomber Command was then ploughing through the main centres of population must have made such an outcome seem likely to those who occupied them. All the same nowhere during the Battle of Berlin was anything approaching the scale of destruction and loss of life caused in Hamburg in July to August 1943, achieved. Nowhere in the Battle of Berlin would Bomber Command achieve again an attack so accurate and so concentrated as those which had brought ruin and chaos to Hamburg.

Unlike the Battle of the Ruhr, which began shortly after the introduction to operations of the Oboe equipped Mosquito and the Battle of Hamburg which saw the first surprise use of window and which offered H_2S a virtually unique opportunity, the Battle of Berlin opened without special advantages for Bomber Command. The limitations of H_2S blind marking had not been overcome. The range of Oboe could not yet be extended to reach Berlin or other targets beyond the Ruhr. The Germans had become familiar with window. The generally long range of the attacks gave their fighters the maximum time in which to react and the heavy concentration on Berlin itself all too often gave them an obvious clue as to where to go. Berlin too was an especially bad H_2S target because the size of it flooded the screen and it was naturally packed with intense anti-aircraft gun and searchlight defences.

THE RUHR

0　Miles　20
0　Kilometres　30

Independent Mosquito night operations January 1943 - April 1945

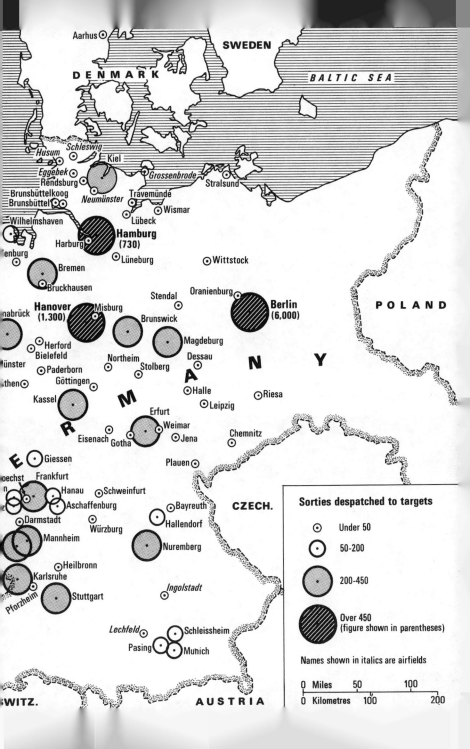

Aarhus ⊙

SWEDEN

DENMARK

BALTIC SEA

Husum ⊙ *Schleswig*
Eggebek ⊙ Kiel ⊙ *Grossenbrode*
Rendsburg ⊙ *Stralsund*
Brunsbüttelkoog *Neumünster* Travemünde
Brunsbüttel ⊙⊙ *Wismar*
Wilhelmshaven ⊙ Lübeck
⊙ Harburg **Hamburg**
enburg **(730)**
⊙ Lüneburg ⊙ Wittstock

⊙ Bremen
Bruckhausen

Stendal Oranienburg ⊙
nabrück **Hanover** Misburg **POLAND**
(1,300) Brunswick **Berlin**
⊙ Herford ⊙ Magdeburg **(6,000)**
Bielefeld Northeim Dessau
ünster ⊙ Paderborn Stolberg ⊙
then Göttingen ⊙ Halle N
Kassel ⊙ Leipzig ⊙ Riesa

Erfurt Y
Weimar
Eisenach Gotha Jena Chemnitz
E ⊙ Giessen Plauen ⊙
oechst Frankfurt
n Hanau ⊙ Schweinfurt CZECH.
Aschaffenburg ⊙ Bayreuth
⊙ Darmstadt Würzburg Hallendorf
Mannheim
⊙ Heilbronn Nuremberg
Karlsruhe
Pforzheim Stuttgart *Ingolstadt*

Lechfeld Schleissheim
Pasing Muhich

Sorties despatched to targets

⊙ Under 50

⊙ 50-200

⊙ 200-450

◆ Over 450
(figure shown in parentheses)

Names shown in italics are airfields

SWITZ. AUSTRIA

| 0 | Miles | 50 | 100 |
| 0 | Kilometres | 100 | 200 |

Above and below: High performance Focke-Wulf night fighters
Right: 88mm Anti-Aircraft Gun

Above all and in spite of ever increasingly ingenious feint tactics and radio deceptive measures, the Germans became more and more successful in feeding their night fighters into the dense Bomber Command streams en route to and from their targets. Once the contact was made the fight was unequal. The British bombers were, of course, completely outclassed by the German fighters in performance and they were also heavily outgunned by them. Once the bombers were under attack, they had little hope of survival beyond mistakes which might be made by the German pilots and, in the Ju 88s and Me 110s, their observers. The bombers had to carry vast loads of 100 octane petrol, high explosive and incendiary bombs and scarcely less dangerous oxygen bottles to keep the crews conscious. Highly explosive and highly inflammable, they were veritable tinder boxes. While many of their crews must have died lingering deaths of several minutes duration, many others must have disintegrated before they knew what had hit them. There is no doubt that among the 1,047 bombers which went down in the Battle of Berlin, the greatest executioners by far were the German night fighters.

Efforts to deceive them occasionally succeeded. For example, on the night of 5th February 1944, Bomber Command's target was Stettin. The 358 bombers ordered to attack it were routed in such a way that on their final leg they were pointing not only at Stettin but also Berlin. About twenty minutes before zero hour at Stettin, some Mosquitoes arrived over Berlin and began to drop markers as if a main attack was about to develop. The German fighter controllers marshalled their forces over Berlin and several lanes of fighter flares were laid to show up the heavy bombers which meanwhile were completing their runs across Stettin. A great and increasing variety of other deceptive measures were taken including the use of the German night fighter wave-lengths to broadcast bogus instructions to their pilots. More often than not and more and more often, the German fighters all the same found the bomber stream. The longer the Battle of Berlin lasted the higher became the casualties. Moreover, this was so in spite of the fact that in the later stages Bomber Command concentrated less on Berlin and tried to spread the German defences by constant shifts in the focus of the attacks.

All these and other tactical innovations no doubt delayed and made harder the ultimate success of the German night fighters. They did not however prevent it and by the beginning of April 1944, Harris warned the Air Staff that 'remedial action' of another and a more radical kind was urgently necessary. He believed that Bomber Command was in need of night fighter support 'on a substantial scale'.

So, instead of finishing the war in the Battle of Berlin, Bomber Command, despite its huge effort, painful endeavour and brave sacrifice, clinched a different matter. Ultimately, the cover of darkness did not avail. Bomber Command originally took to it to escape the German fighters but discovered that in it they could not find their targets. The means which they then developed to find targets in the dark also, broadly, availed the German fighters to find them and so now they could not escape the night fighters. Thus, to concentrate their attacks for long enough upon targets of sufficient importance to give them a chance of achieving decisive results, Bomber Command was exposed to casualty rates beyond what could be afforded and endured. In the Battle of Berlin, Bomber Command reached the unacceptable level of casualties but the effects of the bombing, painful and damaging as they were to Germany, did not even approach decisive proportions.

No man can say how Germany would have fared if Bomber Command had not mounted its great area

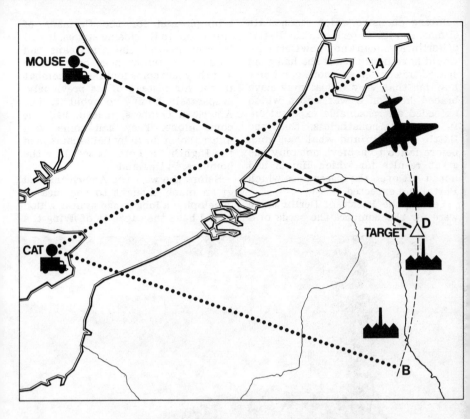

Oboe
Signals were transmitted from the 'Cat' and 'Mouse' stations.
These were boosted by equipment in the aircraft and received again by the
Cat and Mouse. Thus the distance of the aircraft from the two transmitters
was measured. In this way the aircraft was kept on a track of constant distance
from the Cat (A.B). When it reached a pre-calculated distance from the
Mouse (C.D) it was over the target

bombing offensive which reached its climax and its Waterloo in the Battle of Berlin. None can know how Germany would have flourished if she had been spared this ordeal and none can know how far that very ordeal may have braced her for a war effort which exceeded all reasonable expectation. It is clear, nonetheless, that the Battle of Berlin and what had gone before failed to achieve not only the great results for which Harris had hoped but even the lesser ones which Portal had expected.

Yet, in the Battle of Berlin there were for the bombers the seeds of a triumph and for the Germans of ruination. In its closing stages, it will be remembered, the Americans had made four appearances over Berlin and they had come looking for combat in the air instead of, as previously, desperately hoping to avoid it. The American bombers, indeed, had not come alone. They had come with fighter cover flown by P51 Mustangs of the Eighth Air Force based, like the bombers, in England.

Before the war, the Americans had given much thought to the idea of developing a long range fighter which would have the capacity of flying the

same distance as long range bombers. When it came to the point of going into action, however, the United States Army Air Forces had no long range fighters. The difficulty of developing such a thing and the impressive performance and great fire power of the B17 Flying Fortress bombers combined as factors leading to the conclusion that day bombing, despite the British and German experiences in 1939 and 1940, would be possible without protective fighter cover. After the initial daylight experiments which the Americans carried out over France in 1942, they tended to become more and more the victims of their own propaganda. The exaggerated claims of what the Fortresses shot down and the fact that their initial targets were not heavily defended by the Germans combined as factors leading to the rejection of Portal's opinion that the idea of the self-defending bomber formation would not work and the rejection of it, in turn, led Portal to abandon the opinion. He realised that the

P47 Thunderbolt. The pilot is Lieutenant-Colonel F E Gabreski, who became the leading US ace

OCT 16 1943 ©C1B 603324

The Was

The Weather

Today — Intermittent light rain and cooler. Yesterday—High, 75; low, 56. (Details on Page B-9.)

O.24,592   Entered as Second Class Matter, Postoffice, Washington, D. C.   Copyright, 1943, By The Washington Post.   WASHINGTON: FRI

0 Forts Lost, 104 Nazi
Yanks Pour Tanks In
Zaporozhe Falls, 10

---

ouse Group ould Ban l Subsidies fter 1943

resent Programs lay Run to Dec. 31, House Banking Committee Says

Vegetable Ceilings

LING PRICES put on 13 winr vegetables. Page 5.

Fight Coming

By Robert C. Albright
Post Staff Writer

e House Banking Committee rday aimed another knock-low at the Administration's mer subsidy program, re with watertight language cally the same legislation dent Roosevelt vetoed earlier ear.

committee approved the ned subsidy prohibitions, 16 before reporting a bill ex g the life of the Commodity t Corp. another 18 months. endment by Representative tt (Republican) of Michigan, ded the ban on consumer ents to all Federal agencies. ven committee Republicans d with one Progressive and Democrats to clamp down the ctions which Administration ers charged would shoot liv-

---

95,000 on the Books

Draft Delinquents Face Induction After Nov. 1

(New manpower regulations, as they affect Federal workers, explained in Jerry Kluttz' Federal Diary on Page B-1.)

By Ben W. Gilbert
Post Staff Writer

Selective Service yesterday ordered the country's 6500 local draft boards to reclassify into 1-A for immediate induction into the armed forces all draft delinquents aged 18 through 37 after November 1.

The action in effect set up a Nation-wide dragnet to catch an estimated 95,000 draft delinquents now on the books and send them into the armed services or make them stand trial for violation of the Selective Service Act.

Delinquents failing to respond to induction orders will be reported to the Department of Justice for arrest and prosecution. Violations of draft regulations may be punished by a maximum fine of $10,000 and five years in prison.

Selective Service defined draft delinquents as persons who had failed to keep the local board informed of an address where mail will always reach them and other variations of failing to keep in touch with local boards including:

Failure to return a completed Selective Service questionnaire within 10 days.

Giving false information in the questionnaire.

Failure to register.

Failure to report a change of status which would affect classification.

Failure to report for physical examination.

Failure to report for induction (or for work of national importance in the case of conscientious objectors.)

Selective Service pointed out that it was setting up a continuing program designed to reduce the number of delinquents—in fairness to men in the armed forces and fathers about to be inducted. Previously, draft delinquency cases

See DRAFT, Page 6, Column 2

Strong Peace Policy Group Asks Hearing

Senate advocates of a strong Senate foreign policy declaration yesterday demanded a hearing be-

---

U. S. Divisions Rally Support In Fund Drive

As Coleman Jennings, chairman of the Community War Fund drive for $4,800,000, called upon cam-

---

Brewster Trouble La To Labor I

Federal Legisla Prevented Their 'Getting Tough,' Witnesses Indica

By Mary Spargo
Post Staff Writer

Hard-pressed Navy fighting off charges of an "umbrella policy" at th ster Aeronautical Corp. yesterday indicated stron the whole structure of lation and Government la cies had prevented their tough about production of and fighters to prosecute.

This line of defense a vigorously conducted attac House Naval Affairs subc investigating Brewster's p was implicit in hours of t from ducking officials, wh away from the issue as they hit it.

Determined committee led by the quietly inflexib man Drewry (Democrat ginia, indicated that the c revealed at the Brewste were so shocking that the tee might launch an inve into other plants holding N tracts.

Bard Summarizes Trouble

Assistant Secretary of Ralph A. Bard led off in N investigating yesterday with a su

ngton Post

Washington Merry-Go-Round

For an exciting column on happenings in official Washington, read Drew Pearson's "Washington Merry-Go-Round" daily in The Post.

OCTOBER 15, 1943   X★★★★   DISTRICT OF COLUMBIA AND SUBURBAN AREA   **THREE CENTS**

lanes Downed in Raid;
Broken Volturno Line
,000 Periled in Crim

Reds Smash 3 German Divisions In Breakthrough North of Kiev

By the Associated Press

London (Friday), Oct. 15.—The Red army captured the Dnieper River bend stronghold of Zaporozhe yesterday, sealed off Melitopol for early conquest and cut its railway link with the Crimea, and in a new breakthrough north of Kiev smashed three German divisions, Moscow announced early today.

The fall of the east bank industrial citadel of Zaporozhe opened the way for a Soviet landslide southward into the Crimea, where 100,000 German troops risk encirclement. Front dispatches said Soviet units already were pursuing German remnants from the broken Zaporozhe-Melitopol line.

Nearly 10,000 Germans were slain as the Russians overwhelmed Zaporozhe's desperate Nazi garrison, and fought their way toward early triumphs at Kiev, on the middle Dnieper, and at Gomel in White Russia.

Tanks Lead Breakthrough

The Germans, still throwing their precious reserves into the inferno raging on both sides of Kiev, lost 3000 men in one area there. 3000 at Zaporozhe, 1500 at Gomel and 2000 at Melitopol, on the basis of preliminary data, said Moscow's midnight broadcast communique supplement, recorded by the Soviet monitor here.

"In the area north of Kiev," it added, "our tanks broke through German positions and smashed three enemy divisions."

Allies Storm Forward
Furious Night Assault Cracks River Defense

By Edward Kennedy
Associated Press Staff Writer

Allied Headquarters, Algiers, Oct. 14.—The Germans' first natural defense line before Rome—the steep-banked Volturno River—has been smashed by the Fifth Army at several points near Capua in a furious night assault in which Allied engineers bridged the stream under withering German fire. Allied headquarters announced today.

American and British infantry and armored forces, including tanks, stormed across the river in darkness early yesterday after having repelled a futile Nazi assault on Capua, and today were fighting fiercely to expand their bridgeheads against desperate enemy resistance.

So murderous was the aerial cover given Lieut. Gen. Mark W. Clark's attacking troops that Germany's infantry was pinned down to its defensive positions north of the Volturno and not a single Nazi tank was able to join the battle.

There was no exact information

how far Allied vanguards had penetrated beyond the river, but an official announcement that bridgeheads had been firmly established indicated Clark's troops had pushed northward far enough to insure them against German counterattacks.

Throughout today a stream of Allied tanks, artillery, supplies and men rumbled over the makeshift bridges, braving heavy Nazi fire, to support the advance units that were fanning out along the Volturno's northern shore.

Weltering under the sledgehammer blows of Clark's fighters, the Germans are falling back toward the Garigliano River and the Aurunci and Ausoni Mountains. There they undoubtedly will make another stand to delay the invaders again and permit the Germans to hold on to Rome as long as possible.

(A Berlin broadcast said, seaborne British troops, following

See ITALY, Page 11, Column 1

Two U.S. F
Craft Miss
Big Schwei
Plant Wree

By the Associated

London (Friday), C Flying Fortresses r into Germany yesterd the important ball b at Schweinfurt and a number of 60 bombers ing down 91 fighters probably the fierces battle ever fought.

Escorting Thunde fighters—accounted f into Germany, boosting the emy losses to 104. American fighters v boosting the raiders to 62.

The size of the atta was not announced, States Army headqua to them as "large fo

It was the second months at the indu south-central German

The heaviest previ loss was 59 bombers burg-Schweinfurt sh Africa August 17,

600 U. S. Fliers Lost

The RAF peak los ers in the August Berlin. The Germa worst day was Septe when 185 Nazi plan in the Battle of Brit

The American los 600 American flier missing and perhap dollars worth of pre and fighting machine

But preliminary cated that the plant ucts form key part man war machin, was

Yank Fliers Down 12 Zeros In Kahili Raid

By the Associated Press

Allied Headquarters, Southwest Pacific (Friday), Oct. 15.—In a new raid on Kahili, Japan's chief air-

Army Getting Deadly New Superbombers

By Sterling F. Green
Associated Press Staff Writer

A new American super-bomber hauling more explosives and hav-

Americans meant to do day bombing or nothing. In 1943 it began to look more as if it would be nothing. The Eighth Air Force simply could not get effectively and on a sustained basis into the bombing offensive. The generals and especially the one commanding the Eighth Air Force, Eaker, insisted that the main reason was lack of reinforcements. Self-defending formations, they explained, depended for self-defence upon massive fire-power which could only be generated in large formations and, of course, there was something in this. All the same, it was not the real and fundamental cause of the trouble. The Germans could break the formations up by lobbing rockets into them from their heavy fighters, which they called *Zerstörer* (destroyers) and then close in for the kill with machine gun and cannon. To this the American air generals seemed to have no answer nor, despite the appearance of the medium range P47 Thunderbolt fighter, did they seem much concerned with the development of fighter range. It was, strangely enough, a civilian who introduced a new line of action.

In the summer of 1943 Mr Robert A Lovett, the American Assistant Secretary of War for Air, toured the Eighth Air Force bomber bases in England. What he saw and heard evidently made a profound impression and on his return to the United States, he urgently pressed upon General Arnold, the supreme American Air officer, that long range fighters must be brought into action to save the long range bombers. He suggested longer range tanks for Thunderbolts and he said Lightnings and Mustangs would be needed too. Eventually, in July 1943, Arnold told Lovett that the best solution lay in the Mustang, or to be more precise, the P51B development of it. All the same, only 180 of these machines were ordered to England.

The American daylight bomber offensive reached Berlin in May 1944 with devastating effects

Aircraft are strange birds and the distinctions between them which render the differences between brilliant success, useful value and outright failure are often hard to see and more often impossible to predict. So too the effect of modification and redevelopment sometimes produces the most unpredictable and the most surprising results. In these respects and in others, the North American P51 Mustang perhaps, in the Second World War, stands in a class of its own. Its origin was in 1940 when America was still neutral and the British Purchasing Commission there was anxious, for obvious reasons, to acquire almost any aircraft. Finding an opening, they placed an order for Curtiss fighters with the North American Aviation Inc. The firm, however, preferred to offer a new design and, in consultation with the British, the NA Mustang prototype was produced within eighteen weeks. The United States Air Corps, as it then was, tested two models of this machine, found it unimpressive and placed no order, but the hard-pressed Royal Air Force immediately placed an order. Series production was put in hand and in November 1941 the RAF received its first operational Mustangs. It then seemed that the American Air Corps had been right. The Mustang developed a maximum speed of 366 mph at 15,000 feet. It was not good enough to reinforce the Spitfires of Fighter Command. It was unloaded upon Army Cooperation Command, truly the Cinderella of the Royal Air Force. As such, it was used by the British in the Dieppe Commando raid during the summer of 1942.

In October 1942 an experiment was tried with five Mustangs. Their Allison engines were replaced by Rolls Royce Merlins. The initial results were not good but further modifications produced the P51B version which had a differed airframe and a Packard-Merlin engine (Rolls-Royce Merlin built under licence by Packard in the United States). Now the Mustang

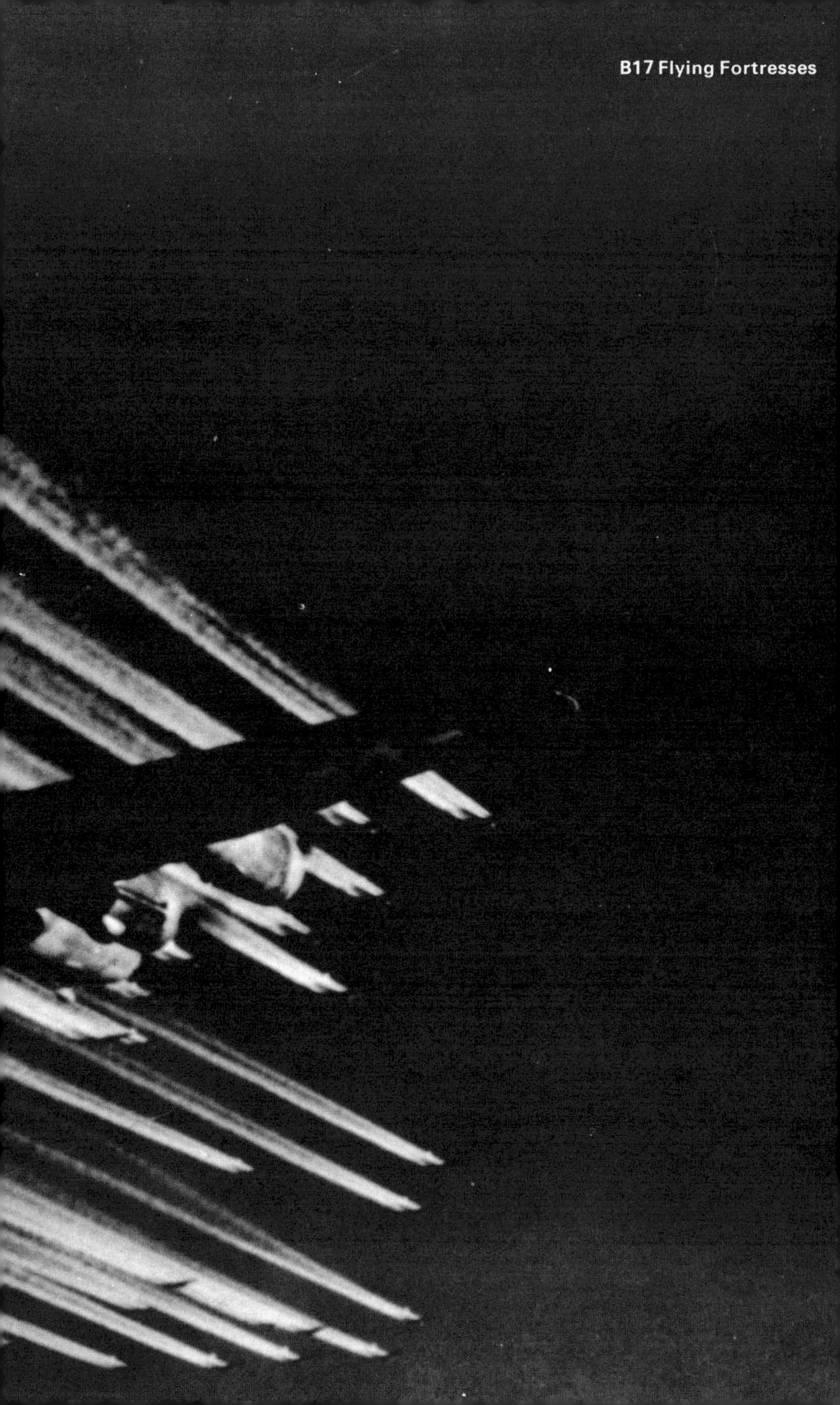
B17 Flying Fortresses

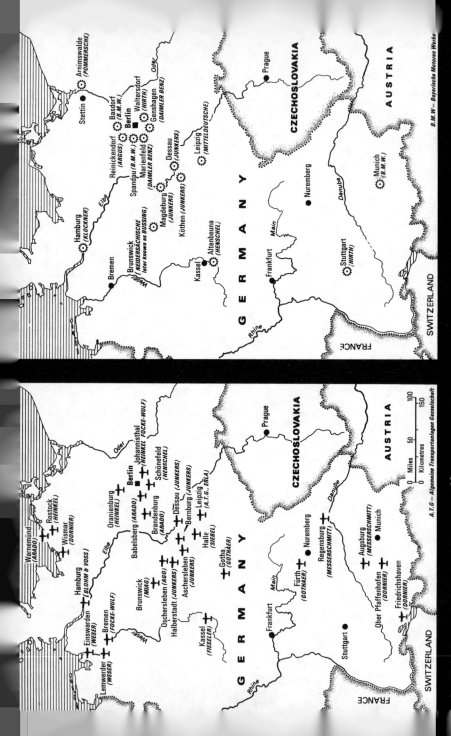

Left: Main German aircraft plants before 1939. *Right:* Main German aero-engine factories before 1939

Right map (aircraft plants):

Warnemünde (ARADO)
Rostock (HEINKEL)
Wismar (DORNIER)
Einswarden (WESER)
Hamburg (BLOHM & VOSS)
Lemwerder (WESER)
Bremen (FOCKE-WULF)
Brunswick (MIAG)
Oschersleben (AGO)
Halberstadt (JUNKERS)
Aschersleben (JUNKERS)
Kassel (FIESELER)
Oranienburg (HEINKEL)
Babelsberg (ARADO)
Brandenburg (ARADO)
Berlin
Johannisthal (HEINKEL FOCKE-WULF)
Schönefeld (HENSCHEL)
Dessau (JUNKERS)
Bernburg (JUNKERS)
Halle (SIEBEL)
Leipzig (A.T.G. ERLA)
Gotha (GOTHAER)
Fürth (GOTHAER)
Regensburg (MESSERSCHMITT)
Augsburg (MESSERSCHMITT)
Munich
Ober Pfaffenhofen (DORNIER)
Friedrichshafen (DORNIER)
Nuremberg
Stuttgart
Frankfurt
Prague

GERMANY
CZECHOSLOVAKIA
AUSTRIA
SWITZERLAND
FRANCE

Elbe
Oder
Weser
Rhine
Main
Danube

0   50   100   Miles
0   50   100   150   Kilometres

A.T.G. = Allgemeine Transportanlagen Gesellschaft

Left map (aero-engine factories):

Arnimswalde (POMMERSCHE)
Stettin
Hamburg (KLÖCKNER)
Bremen
Brunswick (NIEDERSÄCHSISCHE later known as BÜSSING)
Basdorf (B.M.W.)
Waltersdorf (HIRTH)
Genshagen (DAIMLER BENZ)
Reinickendorf (ARGUS)
Berlin
Spandau (B.M.W.)
Marienfeld (DAIMLER BENZ)
Magdeburg (JUNKERS)
Köthen (JUNKERS)
Dessau (JUNKERS)
Leipzig (MITTELDEUTSCHE)
Altenbeuna (HENSCHEL)
Kassel
Frankfurt
Nuremberg
Stuttgart (HIRTH)
Prague
Munich (B.M.W.)

GERMANY
CZECHOSLOVAKIA
AUSTRIA
SWITZERLAND
FRANCE

Elbe
Oder
Weser
Rhine
Main
Danube

B.M.W. = Bayerische Motoren Werke

leapt to the fore as an interceptor fighter. Its speed developed from 375 mph at 5,000 feet to 455 mph at 30,000 feet and even 440 mph at 35,000 feet. This was much better at all heights than the best German equivalents, the Focke-Wulf 190 and the Messerschmitt 109G. But this new Mustang was also of superior manoeuvrability to the German fighters in all respects such as diving, turning and so on, with the single exception of the rolling rate, in which the FW190 excelled. This however, was only half the point. The Mustang, in sharp distinction to the Spitfire, demonstrated a remarkable ability to receive external 'drop' tanks and still to perform well. With two drop wing tanks which gave it a range of nearly 1,500 miles, it lost only about 35 mph. Allowing for dropping the extra tanks before combat and allowing for extra fuel consumption in combat, this would enable Mustangs to fly operationally as cover for bombers up to 600 miles from base. This meant that they could go as far as Berlin and nearly a hundred miles beyond Schweinfurt. This capacity was shown to exist by September 1943 but it was not until after the Schweinfurt disaster of 14th October that sufficiently drastic action was taken to realise it. The Americans then made no mistake. By the end of the war, 14,000 Mustangs were produced. They came into operational service with the Eighth Air Force in December 1943 and by March 1944 they had worked up sufficient range, as has already been mentioned, to afford the daylight bombers cover during their attacks on Berlin.

American air power indeed had recovered with a vengeance. In November 1943 a new American strategic air force based in Italy had been activated. Its role was to continue air operations, previously carried out by tactical air forces, in support of military operations in Italy, but its primary purpose was to initiate strategic bombing of targets in southern Europe such as the Rumanian oil plants at Ploesti and the aircraft factories at Wiener-Neustadt which were either out of or at extreme range from British bases. On 1st January 1944 this new air force and the Eighth in England were placed under the supreme and unified command of General Carl Spaatz and jointly formed into the United States Strategic Air Forces in Europe (USSTAF).

On 20th February 1944 Spaatz launched a series of massive air operations which have since become famous as 'Big Week'. In the first attack more than 1,000 bombers and masses of fighters, long, medium and short range, were despatched. The object was to engage the Luftwaffe on the ground by bombing its factories and in the air by intercepting its fighters and any other aircraft encountered. And at last the Americans had the means of doing so. The changed situation was straight away reflected by the fact that from this armada, only twenty-one of the bombers failed to return.

Sometimes, much worse casualties than this were suffered. For example, from some 430 bombers which got through to their targets on 22nd February, forty-one were shot down or otherwise destroyed. The Germans sprang a surprise on this occasion. Before the advent of the Mustangs, they had usually been able to hold off until the American bombers reached the limit of their fighter cover range. Now that they could not do this they suddenly struck early in the American outward flight. Though they scored an impressive success this also revealed an unfavourable tendency for the Germans. They had lost their safe zones for intercepting the Fortresses. They now had to strike wherever and whenever they could. The Mustangs forced them to do that. So all the other American and British fighters, the Lightnings, Thunderbolts and even the Spitfires began to get chances of engaging the Germans.

The battle of Berlin

Unsere Mauern brechen, aber unsere Herzen nicht!

In these tremendous air battles of February 1944, brought on by Eighth and Fifteenth Air Force bombers from England and Italy, targets all over Germany and Austria from Steyr, Augsburg, Stuttgart and Regensburg in the south, Schweinfurt, Gotha and Leipzig in the centre, to Brunswick, Diepholz and Rostock in the north were bombed. Heavy damage was done to numerous aircraft, ball bearing and other plants, but more important than this was that the Americans began to get the upper hand in the combats with the German fighters. So much so that from March onwards, General Spaatz adopted more and more the tactics of forcing the Luftwuffe to action rather than, as previously, of trying to get to and fro surreptitiously and with the minimum contact with the enemy air force. Thus, the command of the daylight air over Germany began in February and March 1944 to swing decisively away from the Germans and in favour of the Americans. The writing on the wall for the Germans was that in March 1944 American bombers, undertaking very deep penetrations of Germany day after day, lost 3·5 per cent of their number which got through to their targets. In October 1943 this loss rate had been 9·1 per cent.

This development changed the prospect of the war in the air and so too of the war altogether. It did not save Bomber Command from its tribulations in the night offensive yet awhile, but in combination with other factors, it was soon to be an important relieving factor in that problem too.

Above: A Lancaster down in Germany. *Below:* Me 110

Above: The Overlord High Command. Left to right, General Omar Bradley (US 12th Army Group), Admiral Sir Bertram Ramsey (Naval Forces), Air Marshal Sir Arthur Tedder (Deputy Supreme Commander), General Dwight D Eisenhower (Supreme Commander), General Sir Bernard Montgomery (21st Army Group), Air Marshal Sir Trafford Leigh-Mallory (Air Forces), General Walter Bedell-Smith (Chief of Staff)
Left: Lieutenant-General Carl A Spaatz Commander US Strategic Air Forces
Right: Air Vice-Marshal N H Bottomley
Far right: Group Captain G L Cheshire VC

P38 Lightning

RAF Mustangs

Vickers Wellington II
Engines: Two Rolls-Royce Merlin X, 1,075 hp. *Armament:* Four .303-inch
Browning machine guns and up to 4,000 lbs of bombs. *Maximum speed:* 270 mph at
17,750 feet. *Ceiling:* 23,500 feet. *Range:* 2,200 miles max. *Weight empty:* 22,258 lbs..
Weight loaded: 33,000 lbs. *Span:* 86 feet 2 inches. *Length:* 64 feet 7 inches

Boeing B-17F
Engines: Four Wright R-1820-97, 1,200 hp. *Armament:* Ten or eleven .50-inch
machine guns and up to 8,000 lbs of bombs. *Maximum speed:* 299 mph at 25,000 feet.
Ceiling: 37,500 feet. *Range:* 1,300 miles with 6,000 lbs bomb load, 2,880 miles max.
Weight empty: 34,000 lbs. *Weight loaded:* 55,000 lbs-56,500 lbs. *Span:* 103 feet
9 inches. *Length:* 74 feet 9 inches

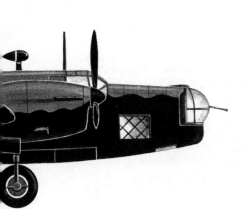

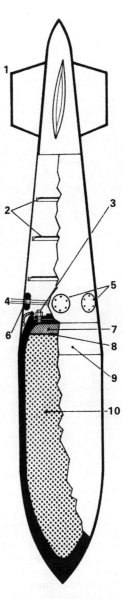

Deep Penetration Bomb of the Grand
Slam (22,000lb – 25' 5" high) and Tallboy
(12,000lb – 21' 0" high) type. 1. Fins
offset 5 degrees to cause spin to bomb.
2. Struts. 3. Exploder container.
4. 3 arming wires. 5. Access doors.
6. Arming wire fairlead. 7. Woodmeal/
wax. 8. TNT topping. 9. Cowling. 10.
Torpex.

P-51 Mustang

One of the classic fighters of the Second World War, the North American P-51 Mustang was originally designed for the RAF, but was so successful, especially when the design was married to a Merlin engine, that it was adopted by the USAF also. Used in a multitude of roles, it found a special niche for itself in that of a long range escort fighter. Specification for P-51 B Mustang: *Engine:* Packard V-1650 Merlin 1,620hp. *Armament:* four .5-inch Browning machine guns (as escort). *Maximum speed:* 440mph at 30,000 feet. *Climb rate:* 3.6 minutes to 10,000 feet. *Maximum range:* 2,200 miles. *Ceiling:* 42,000 feet. *Weights empty/loaded:* 6,840/ 11,200 pounds. *Span:* 37 feet 0¼ inch. *Length:* 32 feet 3 inches.

Armstrong Whitworth Whitley

The first of the RAF's 'heavy' bombers to go into service, and did much valuable work at the beginning of the war. With the arrival of larger, faster and better armed aircraft, however, it was relegated to second line duties such as parachute training. Specification for Whitley Mk V: *Engines:* two Rolls Royce Merlin Xs, 1,075hp. *Armament:* five .303-inch machine guns and up to 3,500 pounds of bombs. *Maximum speed:* 230mph at 16,400 feet. *Climb rate:* 16 minutes to 15,000 feet. *Maximum range:* 2,400 miles. *Ceiling:* 26,000 feet. *Weights empty/loaded:* 19,350/ 33,500 pounds. *Span:* 84 feet. *Length:* 70 feet 6 inches

Avro Lancaster

Undoubtedly the most famous British bomber of the war. Developed from the unsuccessful Manchester, the Lancaster was used in extremely large numbers, and proved capable of carrying enormous bomb loads. Specification for Avro Lancaster B 3: *Engines:* four Packard Merlins, 1,280hp. *Armament:* eight .303-inch Browning machine guns and up to 18,000 pounds of bombs (special variants could carry a 22,000 pound bomb). *Maximum speed:* 275mph at 15,000 feet. *Maximum range:* 2,530 miles with 7,000 pound bomb load. *Weights empty/loaded:* 37,000/ 65,000 pounds. *Span:* 102 feet. *Length:* 69 feet 6 inches.

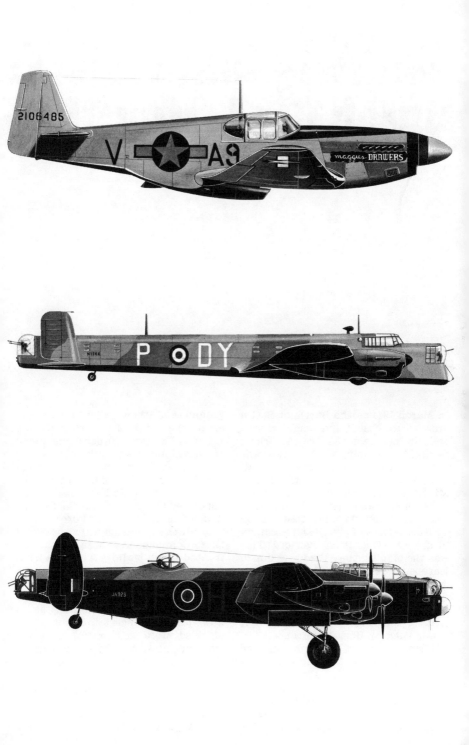

Bombing and victory: March 1944 - May 1945

In March 1944 as the Battle of Berlin drew to its costly and tragic climax and, in contrast, as the American daylight bombing offensive was resumed with fighter cover at all ranges, the attention of the Prime Minister and the President, their governments and their military staffs was increasingly rivetted upon another aspect of the Grand Strategy of the war: Operation Overlord. This was the plan for the Allied invasion of Europe through northern France, the defeat of the German armies in the field and the occupation of Western Germany by the United States, Britain and Free France, or, as it would then be, liberated France.

Already, General Eisenhower had been appointed as the Supreme Commander of the Allied Expeditionary Force. Montgomery had come back from dazzling victories in the Middle East and Sicily to command, under Eisenhower, the assault forces on the ground and then, when they were established, the 21st Army Group. Admiral Ramsay, who had commanded the naval forces at Dunkirk, was now to command the naval forces in Overlord and Air Chief Marshal Sir Trafford Leigh-Mallory had been appointed Commander-in-Chief of the Allied Expeditionary Air Force.

Of all the problems which beset all these Commanders, those which confronted Leigh-Mallory were the least tractable and the position which he occupied was the least enviable. The role of air power in Operation Overlord was uncertain and discussions as to how best the uncertainty might be clarified were seldom far removed from disputes. All the same, though the role of the air was controversial, the invasion was certain to fail unless it could in some manner be effectively discharged.

The main dangers which threatened the Anglo-American invaders were

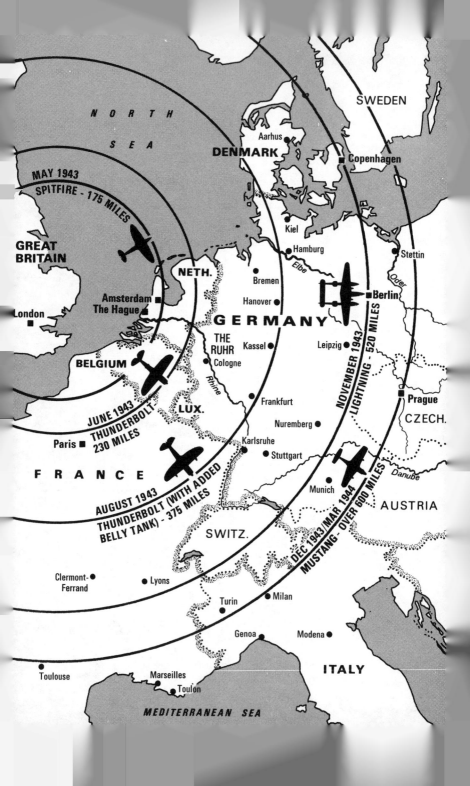

these: first the armies had to be embarked, taken over the sea, disembarked and there married to their equipment, such as tanks and artillery, and supplies, such as food, fuel and ammunition. During these processes they would be at their most vulnerable and if the Germans could effectively attack from the air at the right times the result for the British and Americans might well be disaster. The second main danger arose from the fact that in order to break out of their initial beach-heads and start a continental advance, the Allies had to achieve a local superiority over the German defenders. The British and Americans had to cross the Channel; the Germans could move overland with the assistance of the rail and road communications with which Germany and France were so lavishly equipped. How then could the Allies hope to concentrate faster than the Germans at the vital points? How indeed could they prevent the Germans concentrating so quickly that they would be driven back into the sea before their boots were dry?

The air was the potential answer to both problems. Leigh-Mallory concocted plans for dominating the air over the Channel and the invasion beaches so as to eliminate the risk of the Germans striking at the armada with their air power. He also presented a plan by which German air bases in France would be bombed and the French railway system crippled, also by bombing, before the invasion took place. Thus German air operations on D-Day and thereafter would be further impeded and the German army would be denied its interior lines of communication, or at least an important element in them, and so prevented from concentrating against the invasion forces of General Eisenhower.

The difficulty remained that the air forces assigned to Overlord and placed under Leigh-Mallory's command in the Allied Expeditionary Air Force were inadequate in strength to undertake all these tasks. Some of them,

and especially the preparatory stages of the railway plan, would require heavy bombing. The AEAF, which consisted of light bombers from the United States Ninth and the Royal Air Force Second Tactical Air Forces, fighters from the Air Defence of Great Britain and some transport aircraft, had no authentic heavy bombing capacity. Leigh-Mallory therefore looked to Spaatz and Harris to provide this effort. Neither was anxious to do so.

Spaatz was determined to maintain the newly re-established daylight bombing offensive against Germany and he now argued that the primary targets should be the German synthetic oil plants. He thought the Germans would be bound to defend these at all costs and that if his bombers struck at them, the German fighters would be certain to rise and offer good hunting prospects to his long range fighter pilots. So he hoped to establish more and more firmly an Allied command of the air and so too he hoped to inflict lethal injury upon the German war economy. A shortage of fuel would affect transport, industry and, when it became critical, the armed forces themselves, especially the most mechanised elements such as the Luftwaffe and the Panzer divisions. This Spaatz not only thought but insisted would be a much more useful contribution to Overlord than railway bombing in France or the like. Harris too was very doubtful about the railway plan and he told the Chief of the Air Staff that his bombers would in any case be unable to achieve the necessary aiming accuracy to realise it.

In essence, both Spaatz and Harris had become convinced that the true role of the heavy bombers lay in attacking the heart of Germany strategically. They were anxious to avoid diversions which would directly involve their forces in military operations at the perimeter of Hitler's Europe. Thus, Spaatz wanted to start an oil offensive and keep up the engagement with the German fighter force; Harris wanted to complete the great area attack on German cities which he had been instructed to undertake when he first took up his command in February 1942. Neither was disposed to pay much attention to Leigh-Mallory, a mere fighter commander without, they thought, real understanding of the bombing role.

The *dénouement* came in March. Responding to the firm insistence of Portal upon the point, Harris ordered a series of initially experimental attacks by Bomber Command upon French marshalling yards; the first one took place on the night of 6th March when 261 Halifaxes and six Mosquitoes were despatched to Trappes. The result showed and later evidence further reinforced the lesson that the attacks were much more accurate than the C-in-C had predicted. The railway plan was demonstrated to be a feasible campaign of war.

All the same, there was still opposition to it and not only from General Spaatz. To many, railway bombing seemed unprofitable. If one line was cut, another could be used, and if inconvenience was caused in France, the Germans would ensure that the French and not they were the first to suffer it. Mr Churchill was gravely perturbed by the loss of French life which, however careful and accurate the aim, would be involved in bombing French railway centres.

These questions became the particular concern of the Deputy Supreme Commander, Sir Arthur Tedder, whose experience of commanding air forces in the Middle East and in the invasions of Sicily and Italy gave him unique qualifications to judge them. Tedder was a convinced advocate of the railway plan. It was not a question simply of cutting lines and dislocating sidings, which could easily and rapidly be repaired; it was a question of the systematic destruction by very heavy bombing of the repair facilities and nerve centres of the system. If this could be achieved, then simple cuts in lines and the shooting up of individual trains would be effective because the normal repair and reorganising capacity would already have been removed. Thus, the preparatory attacks by heavy bombers would open the way for tactical operations by light bombers and rocket firing fighters once the invasion had actually taken place. Thus, the potential advantage which the Germans had of operating upon interior lines of communication would be removed.

These considerations and the endorsement they received from General Eisenhower guaranteed the future of the railway plan. The burden of it fell on Bomber Command, to which was allocated more than half the total number of targets to be attacked in the pre-invasion phase. The rest were shared between Leigh-Mallory's AEAF and Spaatz's Eighth Air Force. The operations proved to be of the greatest importance and it can scarcely be doubted that up to that time, namely June 1944, they represented the most immediately successful and profitable bombing attacks on a heavy and sustained scale ever carried out. They produced a growing railway paralysis in northern France which had the immediate effect of slowing down the countermeasures which Rommel had in hand for resisting the Allied landings at the coast and the ultimate one, as designed, of stretching the whole transport system to the point at which it could be and was snapped at vital places during the land battle which followed the landings on 6th June.

Another consequence of the railway campaign was of great importance. This concerned the development of a bombing technique by night which it stimulated. In the opening attacks between the first on 6th March and the fifteenth on 10th April, which involved the despatch of more than 2,500 heavy

Above: The marshalling yards at Tours. *Below:* The marshalling yards at Juvisy before and after attack

bomber sorties to eleven marshalling yards, the general method was to aim from medium height, that is between 8,000 and 14,000 feet, at target markers laid down by Mosquitoes of the Pathfinder Force operating at high altitude on Oboe indications. This resulted in more than half the aircraft despatched dropping their bombs within less than 700 yards of the aiming points. Though this was a remarkable achievement, some thought it not good enough and, in particular, Wing Commander Cheshire who was now the CO of the Dambusters' squadron, was developing a daring system of 'dive' marking.

The marshalling yards at Rennes which were also bombed before D-Day

Using a Mosquito on the night of 5th April he gave an astonishing demonstration of what could be done. Diving to within 1,000 feet or less of an aircraft factory at Toulouse and using not a bombsight but the gunsight, Cheshire fixed his aiming point visually and deposited a red spot fire upon it. This was quickly backed up by more markers conventionally aimed from more comfortable heights. 140 Lancasters of 5 Group then came over and with an absolutely clear aiming point, soon finished off the factory.

This method, which was presently refined still further, immensely increased the accuracy of night attack, as was seen, for example, in the marshalling yards at Tours, Juvisy

and La Chapelle. In fact, it reduced what had been an average error of about 700 yards for half the force despatched (the other half being excluded under the heading of gross errors) to something under 300 yards for the whole force involved. Moreover, this technique aided not only the railway plan, the counter V-bomb campaign and all the other tasks which Bomber Command had over France; it was also found, through the steady nerve of Wing Commander Cheshire, to have effective applications over more heavily defended German targets. The outstanding example of this was provided by the successful attack on Munich on the night of 24th April after which Cheshire was awarded the VC.

Bomber Command was, in fact, developing techniques which were rendering its night operations more accurate than their American counterparts by day. This tendency, allied to what the Americans had now achieved against the German day fighter force and were about to initiate against German oil plants, marked the real beginning of the end for Hitler's Germany. It was the portent of the effective destruction of the heart of a nation already threatened at its frontiers by Stalin's armies from the east, General Alexander's from the south and General Eisenhower's from the west.

On 12th May 1944 some 935 heavy bombers of the Eighth Air Force accompanied, preceded and followed by an armada of American and British fighters, set course for the synthetic oil plants at Zwickau, Merseburg-Leuna, Brüx, Lützkendorf, Bohlen and elsewhere. A severe air action followed in which the Americans lost forty-six bombers, the Americans and the British ten fighters, and the Germans perhaps as many as fifty fighters, perhaps more. All the oil plants aimed at were damaged and some were temporarily put completely out of action. In addition there was, as investigation after the war showed, an unexpected dividend. A building

was hit at Merseburg-Leuna in which heavy water experiments connected with German interest in the atomic bomb were going on. Meanwhile, the Fifteenth Air Force was engaged in a sustained offensive against the oil refineries at Ploesti in Rumania through which Germany had her only access to considerable supplies of natural oil. These initial American strikes against German oil production and supply were quickly followed up and developed and within a few nights of D-Day, Bomber Command joined the same campaign by launching night attacks on the oil plants at Gelsenkirchen, Sterkrade, Wesseling and Scholven.

There were now three main strategic variations on the bombing offensive which might be run in combination or in competition. One was the oil campaign, just initiated. Another was the development of the railway plan to form a grand transportation campaign to do to all Germany what had already been done to northern France. A third was the resumption on a massive scale of the area offensive against German cities.

The outstanding success of the opening American attacks on German oil plants demonstrated impressively one of the new factors in the bombing offensive: the Americans, though not, of course, without loss to themselves, could fight their way through to their chosen targets at greater cost to the enemy than to themselves and, having got through, they could deal out really damaging blows to the objectives, in this case the oil plants. This meant that the Americans were now not only beginning to achieve their strategic aim, that is the destruction of a vital element in the German war economy, but that at each step they were increasing the extent of their air superiority.

The limitations which remained upon the effectiveness of the American contribution to the bombing offensive were the reflection of the very qualities which had produced this success.

After the bombing, survivors begin the long task of clearing up

First, the daylight formations had to be tightly packed and tactically arranged in order to enable them to fight their way to the targets and to avoid the danger of massive destruction from flak they had to operate at very high altitudes. The formation tactics meant that individually aimed attacks were impossible. All the bombardiers dropped their bombs on a signal from the formation leader and they fell in a pattern on the ground which corresponded with the pattern the formation had in the air at the time. This 'pattern' bombing was obviously less accurate than the results which could be achieved by a series of individually aimed attacks such as would occur if each bomb aimer sighted his aiming point and aimed at it. The need for high flying

meant that the attacks, in addition, often had to be made from above cloud on radar indications and the same need had influenced the design of the B17 Flying Fortress to favour high flying as opposed to weight lifting. Thus, per aircraft, American bomb loads were much smaller than the British, and more important, the larger British bombs of 8,000lbs or 12,000lbs could not be carried in Fortresses. For this reason, American inflicted damage on German oil plants proved to be much more readily repairable than the British.

The second great new factor in the offensive was, however, the development of British night bombing techniques which made it possible not only for Bomber Command to join the American assault on oil plants and other targets which required precision attack but to achieve results which often proved to be more precise than

could be achieved by day. Thus, the greater destructive power of Bomber Command became available for the more surgical types of operations which had previously, on a large scale, been more or less the American monopoly.

The limitation which remained here was the continuing high cost of night operations. The German night fighter force had not been brought to action and defeat as the day fighter force had been. Long range night fighters, Beaufighters and Mosquitoes, equipped with elaborate radar aids had some slight success in hunting German night fighters but nothing like the effect which the long range day fighters had achieved could be reproduced at night. The result was that the Bomber Command Lancasters and Halifaxes now suffered more at night than the Fortresses and Liberators did by day. Indeed from the 832 heavy bomber

sorties despatched by Bomber Command in their initial oil operations in June, ninety-three failed to return. This was twice the bomber losses suffered from a larger force against more distinct targets by the Americans in their daylight oil attacks on 12th May.

These continuing high losses at night led in Bomber Command to a reconsideration of day bombing. The sophisticated formation tactics of the Americans could not be attempted by the night experienced British crews, nor were their aircraft suitable for that sort of flying. All the same, daylight attacks over France by Lancasters and Halifaxes operating in loose gaggles with fighter cover proved inexpensive during June, July and August. On 27th August a more ambitious ploy was attempted. More than 200 Halifaxes were despatched in daylight to bomb the oil plant at Homberg. They were accompanied by about 200 Spitfires of Fighter Command. Cloud somewhat interfered with the bombing accuracy but every one of the bombers returned safely to base. The only German aircraft sighted was an Me110 which the Spitfires quickly drove off.

The fact that Spitfires could accompany bombers all the way to the Ruhr was significant of another important new factor in the bombing offensive: the break-out from their Normandy beachheads and the advance across France and towards the German frontier of Eisenhower's Overlord armies. Behind the armies the Allies built or occupied airfields and set up radar transmitters. Thus, the range of the fighters into Germany was extended and thus too the range of the bombers' radar aids both for target finding and for disrupting and deceiving the German night fighters was extended. The German fighter force also, by the same process, lost the whole of its early warning installations and forward bases in France. These factors, combined with the effects of the oil campaign, which by

August were already biting, caused the virtual collapse of the German night fighter force and a further extension of the Anglo-American command of the air which was quickly reflected in a precipitate decline of Bomber Command's casualties. In June 1944 Bomber Command lost 11 per cent of its heavy bomber night sorties despatched to German targets. In August this loss rate fell to 3·7 per cent. In September it fell still further and throughout this period, Bomber Command's day losses, despite the somewhat hastily improvised tactics, never rose to serious dimensions.

A B24 Liberator hit by flak after a raid on Quakenbrück

Indeed, the introduction of daylight bombing in Bomber Command initially turned upon little more than the issue to the aircrews of sun glasses and the general instruction to keep together.

In these ways, the huge destructive potential of the Anglo-American bombing offensive was increasingly liberated. Nor was it only the precision and versatility of it which had been so greatly increased by the improvement in techniques, weapons and aircraft and the reduction of the opposition; the scale of it had also vastly expanded. In July and August 1944 Bomber Command dropped more than 120,000 tons of bombs compared with the 37,000 which it had dropped in the

same two months of 1943. In July and August 1944 the American Eighth Air Force dropped 85,000 tons compared with 7,500 tons in the same months of 1943, and to this, in 1944, had to be added the much smaller but not insignificant contribution of the Fifteenth Air Force from Italy.

The problems of target finding, bomb aiming and effective destruction were being rapidly reduced by the introduction of progressively more efficient techniques, the development of new aids and the production of more powerful bombs ranging eventually to the 12,000lb Tallboy and 22,000lb Grandslam, designed by Dr Barnes Wallis and of unprecedented destructive potential. German Europe was

now a markedly smaller area which reduced the problems of bombing ranges and, of itself, increased the geographical concentration of bombing. Even the tactical air forces supporting the advancing armies now began willy-nilly to make a contribution to the strategic bombing of Germany.

This last consideration was a point which made a particular impression upon Tedder, the Deputy Supreme Commander. In attempting to devise a blueprint for the use of air power in the final phase of the war, Tedder was especially impressed by the virtue of finding policies which could be followed by all air forces whether tactical or strategic, long or short range. He was also searching for a formula which by a single policy would meet all the essential needs and especially those posed by, on the one hand, the idea of an independent strategic air offensive against the vitals of Germany and, on the other, the requirement for air preparation and air support of the advancing armies. This broadminded and far-sighted conception was christened by Tedder the strategy of the common denominator. The policy which in his view met it was an attack upon transportation. The objectives, railways, canals and roads, and their supporting facilities, offered targets for all kinds of attack from rocket firing fighters to the heaviest of heavy bombers since they existed all over enemy territory and ranged from lorries and trains on the move to viaducts, tunnels or canal locks and banks. The product of such a policy would also, in Tedder's view, meet the dual requirement since the systematic dislocation of the German transportation system would impede the operations of the German armies and so help the allied advance. The same result would also impede German industrial activity and so be effective as an expression of the strategic bombing offensive.

Such ideas, however, took inadequate account of the especially attractive prospects of the oil offensive and this was a point particularly apparent not only to Spaatz, to whose efforts and determination the initiation of the oil campaign owed so much, but also to Portal, the Chief of the British Air Staff. By August, it was indeed becoming clear that the attacks on oil plants since May were having a remarkable effect. The loss by the Germans of the small natural oil sources in Poland and their large ones in Rumania to the advancing Russians, made their dependence upon the synthetic plants within their own frontiers almost complete.

Spaatz's and Portal's determination to pursue the oil offensive was nourished by the intelligence reports available to them at the time and it would indeed have been further nourished if they had been able to see the secret reports which Speer was making to Hitler. On 30th August, for example, Speer wrote to Hitler telling him that the hydrogenation oil plants at Leuna, Brüx and Poelitz had been brought to a complete standstill. All the classes of fuel including carburettor, diesel, bottled treibgas, and aviation spirit had suffered drastic reductions in output. Aviation spirit which before the bombing began had been in production at the rate of 175,000 tons a month, amounted in August to only 12,000 tons. Treibgas, previously produced at the equivalent of 37,000 tons per month, fell in August to about 3,000 tons. Diesel fuel, produced before the bombing at nearly 90,000 tons a month, totalled 65,000 tons in August, and carburettor fuel production dropped from 125,000 tons to about 60,000 tons in August.

These dramatic production losses caused by bombing produced for Germany a grim prospect. Speer told Hitler that military operations planned for October would have to be curtailed to save fuel and he foresaw the gravest possible crisis both for industry and the armed forces unless the German air defences could somehow check the Allied bomber attacks

or unless the Allies in the belief that they had done sufficient damage to the oil plants, turned to other targets and so allowed the Germans time to repair the damage.

No one knew better than Albert Speer the true position of Germany's war economy and nothing came to light after the war which showed with greater clarity than his reports to Hitler just how successful the Allied oil campaign was and how mistaken the British and Americans were not to have concentrated a greater proportion of their effort upon it after the initial successes in May and June 1944.

Nevertheless, at the time there seemed to be many other bombing activities which might be more profitable. The Commander-in-Chief, Bomber Command was sceptical of the oil plan which he dubbed, like most of the other plans for selective bombing of particular industries such as ball bearings, transportation and so on, as 'panacea' mongering. He was in any case committed to vast efforts in direct support of the armies and he hoped with the effort left over to resume the general area bombing of the major German cities which had not yet been devastated or which had recovered from earlier attentions.

Harris's belief was, and in the light of past experience it was not a wholly surprising one, that intelligence appreciations showing vulnerable links in the German war economy, such as synthetic oil production, usually turned out to be defective. After the attacks had been made he thought that it generally transpired either that the Germans were less dependent than supposed upon that particular complex or that some substitute arrangements or materials could be found. Often in the past, as for example in the case of ball bearings, this had been so. It was, however, most unfortunate that Harris believed the same of the oil plan since in this case, as subsequently emerged, it was not.

Another aspect of attacking the

German people directly in their cities, which was later to have important consequences, began to attract attention in the summer of 1944. This was a plan, subsequently known as 'Thunderclap' for delivering to Germany a *coup-de-grâce* calculated to end the war when otherwise it might drag on. The conditions thought necessary were those in which the German armies were virtually defeated but when underground or guerilla resistance might persist. In such circumstances an overpowering bombing attack on Berlin or some other city or cities might, it was thought, bring it home once and for all to the Germans that surrender was their only practicable recourse.

The possibility of this being a desirable and necessary course of action came under discussion in the councils of the British and American Chiefs of Staff, though the British Air Staff were not much impressed by the idea. Meanwhile, general area bombing of German towns remained a large part of the policy governing the bombing offensive. The growing division of opinion between Portal and Harris was not about the advisability of area bombing of cities which, under many conditions of weather, was all that was possible; it was about the priority which oil bombing and town bombing should be afforded.

This difference and that between

Fuselage of a crashed B17 is cleared away by German engineers

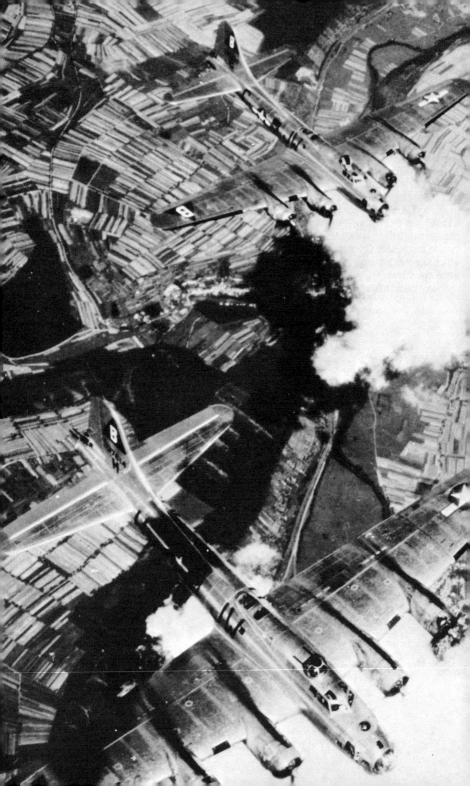

Portal and Harris and Tedder about the bombing policy which ought to be pursued, did not yield to solutions as readily as the tactical and technical problems, which had previously limited the effectiveness of bombing, were doing now. The machinery for directing the bombing offensive was, in short, proving inferior to that which now existed for carrying it out.

In September 1944 the war seemed to be moving towards victory by Christmas. The Russians were approaching the eastern frontiers of Germany, the Anglo-American Allies were moving up Italy and Eisenhower's forces, having liberated France, were closing upon the Rhine. Germany was confronted with an oil famine which threatened to immobilise both her surviving industry and her armed forces. It was, indeed, an open question as to what would be the immediate and operative cause of the disappearance of the Third Reich, strategic bombing or military occupation.

The bombing effort available to achieve the first object or to assist the second was vast. In the last three months of 1944 Bomber Command dropped no less than 163,000 tons of bombs as compared with the 40,000 and 8,000 tons which it had dropped respectively in the last three months of 1943 and 1942. Against a single town, Duisberg, Bomber Command dropped as great a weight of bombs within twenty-four hours as the Germans had brought to bear on London in the whole war. Such was the increase in the British contribution to the combined bomber offensive.

The American contribution, through the Eighth Air Force operating from England and the Fifteenth from Italy, was also growing to formidable proportions. A dramatic and revealing yardstick is provided by considering the (British) tonnages discharged by the three forces in October and November 1944 during which it must be

B17 Flying Fortresses on their way to the target

127

Above: Bomber Command's weapons; general purpose, high capacity, and medium capacity bombs. *Right:* Cluster of American incendiary bombs falls on Kiel. The second container is about to break open

remembered operations were often curtailed by bad weather. These were: Bomber Command: 114,226 tons, Eighth Air Force: 75,033 tons, Fifteenth Air Force: 24,899 tons.

The problem of concentrating this effort on the most profitable targets remained and increased for two main reasons. First, there was the difficulty of deciding upon what they were which, during this period, produced a severe disagreement between the Chief of the British Air Staff, Portal, and the C-in-C Bomber Command, Harris. Secondly, there was the winter weather which interposed obstacles between the aim and the targets, especially in the case of the American high level attacks.

During the last three months of 1944, Bomber Command devoted fifty-three per cent of its tonnage to area attacks on large German cities, fifteen per cent to railways and canals, fourteen per cent to oil plant, thir-teen per cent to direct military targets in support of the armies and five per cent to naval and other targets. In October, the concentration on area bombing of cities had been ever greater, amounting to two-thirds of the effort in that month and that on oil even less, amounting only to six per cent. This led Portal to take up the cudgels with Harris. He expressed his strong belief that oil attacks had the capacity of bringing the war to an early conclusion and also his doubts about the effectiveness of the general area attacks from that point of view. He repeatedly urged Harris to put more effort on to oil and less on to cities. Though Harris was unconvinced there was, nevertheless, a strong upsurge in oil attacks during November when Bomber Command carried out heavy attacks by day and night on the plants at Nordstern, Scholven, Wesseling, Homberg, Wanne Eickel, Sterkrade, Castrop, Kamen, Bottrop

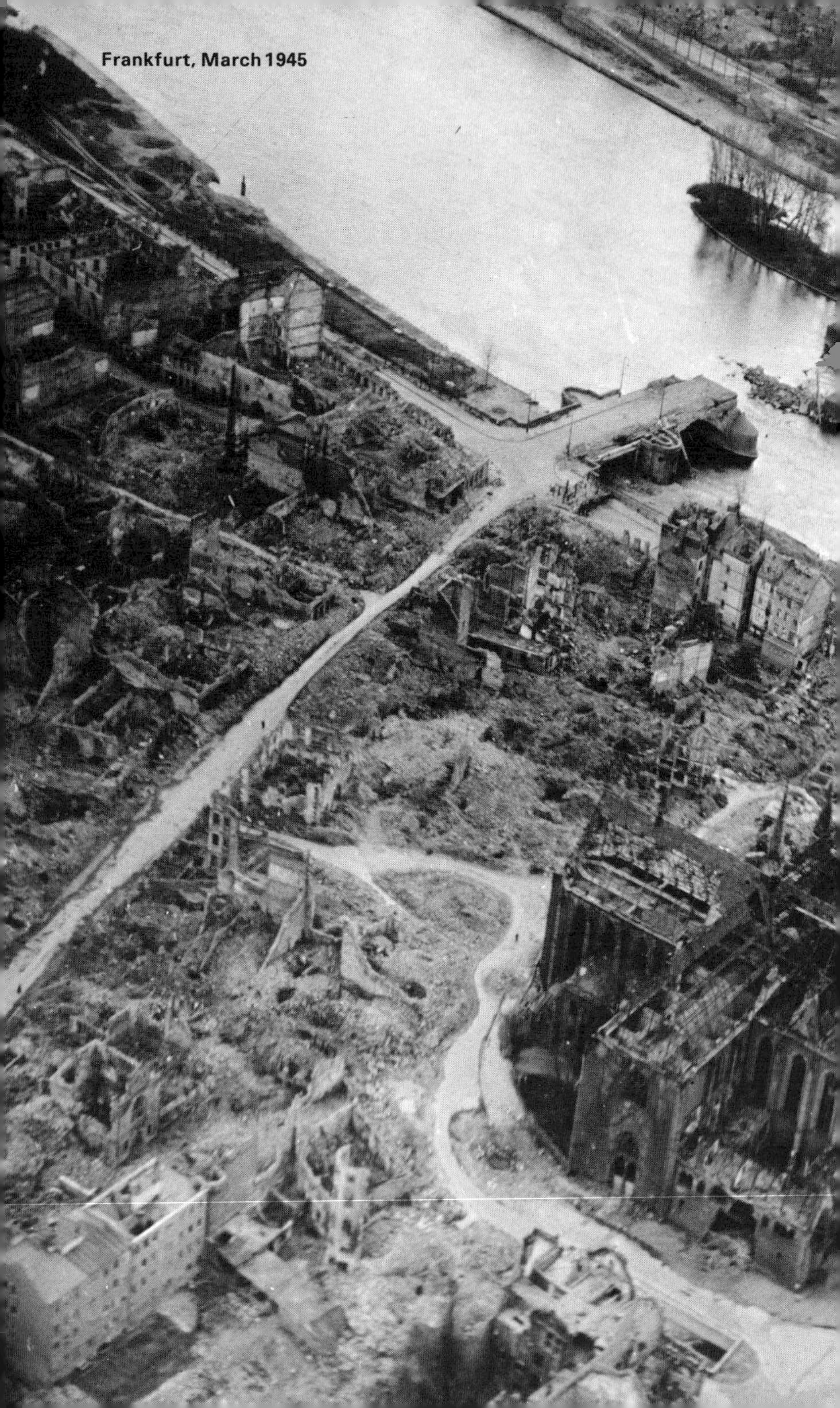
Frankfurt, March 1945

THE RUHR

Hüls

Datteln

EWALD (FORTSETZUNG)

HUGO II
SCHOLVEN

Buer

Gladbeck

CONSOLIDATION

GRAF
BISMARCK

Gelsenkirchen

ALMA PLUTO

GUTEHOFFNUNGSHUETTE

MATHIAS STINNES

PROSPER

Sterkrade
Holten

Bottrop

Bruck-
hausen

RUHROEL
NORDSTERN

Meiderich

Homberg

ERIN

Wanne Eickel

KRUPPS

Castrop
Rauxel

GNEISENAU

KAISERSTUHL

MINISTER STEIN
HOESCH
BENZIN

Dortmund

HANSA
HORDER VEREIN

HARPENERWEG

Dahlbusch

Bochum

ROBERT
MUSER

Essen

CAROLINEN-
GLÜCK

EMIL

BRUCHSTRASSE

Duisburg

Hattingen

| Bochum | = | Town |
| *KRUPPS* | = | Oil Plant |

| 0 | Miles | | 10 |
| 0 | Kilometres | | 20 |

Deschowitz

Blechhammer

Bohumin

Malopolska

Pardubice

Moravska
Ostrava

Oswiecim
Czechowitz

POLAND

Drohobycz

U.S.S.R.

CHOSLOVAKIA

erbaum

Korneuburg

Floridsdorf

Kagran

ienna

Löbau

hwechat

sendorf

Almasfuzito

Szoeny

Petfurdo

Budapest

HUNGARY

A

Lispe

RUMANIA

Brasov

Ploesti

Brazi

Prahova

Caprag

Osijek

Bucharest

Bosanski Brod

Belgrade

Smederevo

Dubova

YUGOSLAVIA

BULGARIA

RIATIC

U.S. 15th AIR FORCE

SEA

ggia

ALBANIA

GREECE

Kucove

and Dortmund. These operations absorbed some 13,000 tons of bombs which amounted to twenty-four per cent of the effort.

The Eighth Air Force made even greater efforts and its Fortresses and Liberators aimed some 14,000 tons of bombs amounting to thirty-nine per cent of their total effort in November at the plants at Gelsenkirchen, Merseburg-Leuna, Castrop, Sterkrade, Hanover, Hamburg, Harburg, Bottrop, Misburg, Bohlen, Zeitz, Lützkendorf and elsewhere. The Fifteenth Air Force also stepped up its oil attacks and, operating sometimes as much as 500 strong, attacked several southern oil plants including those at Florids-dorf, Moosbierbaum, Blechhammer South, Korneuberg, Vienna-Lübau and Linz.

As Spaatz and Portal had expected these attacks were highly effective. While Portal and Harris were corresponding with each other about the merits and demerits of the case, Speer was continuing to send in his secret reports to Hitler. In one dated 19th January 1945 he showed that in December 151,000 tons of aviation, carburettor and diesel fuel had been produced by comparison with the 284,000 tons which would have been turned out under normal conditions. Particularly striking was the deficiency in aviation fuel. Normal production of this would have yielded 107,000 tons. The actual output was 25,000 tons. Stocks were virtually exhausted and Speer was becoming less optimistic about the repair of the damaged plants. He particularly stressed that the heavier bombs used at night, which he said were falling with an extraordinary accuracy, were doing much more permanent damage than the lighter ones which fell in daylight. Even so, Speer was still hoping that a recovery might be effected by about April, provided the air attacks ceased or diminished.

The situation as it existed was indeed grave for Germany. It is virtually beyond doubt that it could already have been fatal if the British and Americans had between June and December 1944 been able to concentrate more exclusively and more persistently on oil targets. This is what Portal thought. The trouble was he had not the means of knowing for sure that he was right.

Portal was by no means alone in expressing dissatisfaction at the course the bombing offensive was taking. From a viewpoint close to Eisenhower's, Tedder was also disquieted. His theory of a common denominator strategy was indeed finding only a somewhat imperfect expression and in October he produced a memorandum in which he sought to draw the disparate elements of air policy into a comprehensive pattern. The centre of this pattern was to be the transportation system of Germany and the particular focus of the plan which he advocated was to be the Ruhr. Tedder indeed now aimed to achieve by bombing the isolation of the Ruhr, which was indeed a common denominator object, since all kinds of air power could be brought to bear upon its attainment and since its execution would fit in with both the industrial undermining of Germany and Eisenhower's military operations which were now threatening the Ruhr.

Tedder may almost have become the victim of his own propaganda to the extent that his enthusiasm for the symmetry and logic of his argument impinged upon his recognition of the realities of a situation in which Spaatz and Portal were convinced that the way to victory lay through oil bombing and in which Harris remained determined to complete the general area offensive in which over the years so much blood and treasure had been invested. All the same Tedder's ideas found increasing expression in the operations of Bomber Command, the Eighth Air Force and the tactical air forces.

On 11th November 1944 Speer

A Mosquito bomber crew

Area bombing leaves the centre of Düren devastated

reported to Hitler that the situation of the Ruhr had reached a critical stage. Already Speer had taken emergency measures to try to restore the situation. 50,000 foreign labourers had been diverted from trench-digging to repairing the transport system in and around the Ruhr. 30,000 more were to be drawn from the armaments industries to repair industrial damage in the Ruhr. Emergency measures were being taken to restore the waterways and the anti-aircraft defences were being stiffened. Even so, Speer admitted that these measures could make little impression on the situation, namely, the loss of the Ruhr to the German war economy. Not only were the Ruhr industries breaking down through direct damage or lack of supplies, but, for the past six weeks, the whole area had become increasingly isolated from the areas in which the production was required.

Here, as in the case of the French railway campaign of March to June 1944 and the oil plan of May to

December 1944, was a third clear example of major identifiable success for the strategic air offensive and, it should be noticed, success measured on the testimony of primary German evidence as opposed to Allied estimates based partly on guesswork and partly on wishful thinking.

Though this could not be fully known in Britain or America at the time, it was thus, in fact, being established that the most effective bombing results were proceeding from the selective operations against oil plants and communications in distinction to the general attacks on large cities. Nevertheless, it has to be recognised that the effectiveness of the selective plans did all the same owe a great deal to the general attacks which continued and which were, indeed, the greater part of Bomber Command's effort in the last three months of 1944.

In this period Bomber Command delivered general area attacks on sixteen Ruhr towns, on eleven more in the south and southwest and five in central or northern Germany. The heaviest attacks fell on Duisburg,

Essen, Cologne and Dusseldorf, at which a total of over 38,000 tons of bombs were aimed. Between the beginning of October and the end of December Bomber Command aimed at and mostly dropped on the Ruhr some 60,830 tons of bombs. Elsewhere the area attacks fell on Ulm, Stuttgart, Karlsruhe, Heilbronn, Freiburg, Ludwigshafen, Saarbrücken, Nuremberg, Munich, Bonn, Coblenz, Bremen, Wilhelmshaven, Brunswick, Osnabrück and Giessen.

In many of these attacks, and especially those on the Ruhr, which had already been ravaged by fire, the greatest proportion of the bombs were high explosive as opposed to the earlier policy of predominantly incendiary bombs. This was to increase structural damage and to make it more permanent in its effects. Further hardship in many German towns was caused by American attacks, which, because of the height of delivery, often also fell generally on towns rather than selectively on oil plants or marshalling yards.

Though Harris's belief that the selective policies were always based on faulty premises and that the only sure way of inflicting really effective damage was by these general area attacks proved itself to be wrong, especially in relation to the oil and transport plans, there is no doubt that both the oil and transport plans owed some of their success to his general operations. The situation in the Ruhr described to Hitler by Speer in November 1944 was due as much and probably much more to Harris's area bombing than to Tedder's transportation plan. Less important but still not unimportant was the fact that Germany's small benzol plants which contributed to her oil supply were often within general industrial areas and in precise positions unknown to Allied intelligence. Countless numbers of them were totally destroyed in general area attacks on the Ruhr and elsewhere.

Though Bomber Command adhered so persistently to the policy of area bombing, which became more and more effective not only because it became heavier and heavier but also because it became more and more accurate and concentrated, the

development of precision techniques by day and night also went on apace. In addition, the weapons to match these skills were forthcoming. Bomber Command's operations against the German battleship *Tirpitz* serve to illustrate the case.

The *Tirpitz*, among the most powerful and modern capital ships afloat anywhere, had long been a thorn in the flesh of the Allied naval staffs. Lying in a Norwegian base, she might, though in fact she seldom did, emerge to threaten Britain's lines of communication with Russia or with America. Her very existence forced the British to keep a battleship fleet ready to engage her which might otherwise have been deployed elsewhere, perhaps in the Pacific. Not surprisingly, therefore, attempts were made from time to time to destroy or at least maim the great vessel. An epic midget-submarine attack in September 1943 did extensive damage and at least some of the repairs were undone in a Fleet Air Arm attack in March 1944. By the summer the time had come to attack again. The ship was now lying in Alten Fjord at almost the extreme northern end of the long Norwegian coast and here she was out of range of Lancaster bombers operating from Britain if they were to return there after the attack. It was therefore decided to make the attempt from the Russian base at Yagodnik in Archangel. Accordingly, on the evening of 11th September thirty-eight Lancasters armed with Tallboy earthquake 12,000lb bombs or smaller Johnnie Walker anti-shipping bombs took off for Russia. One lost its bombs on the way and returned home. Six more crash landed in Russia as they were unable to find or make contact with Yagodnik. Two more reached Yagodnik in a damaged condition. Twenty-seven arrived fit for action. Two Liberators brought the ground crews, a Mosquito arrived to do the

Bomb aimer's view as a Lancaster releases its load

weather reconnaissance over Alten Fjord and another Lancaster came to film the proceedings.

On 15th September, after some bizarre experiences with their Russian hosts, who incidentally charged them 9,239 roubles for their entertainment, and after a reconnaissance by the Mosquito, the twenty-seven operational and the single Film Unit Lancaster took off for Alten Fjord. They came in over the Fjord just before one o'clock in the afternoon to find little cloud and the *Tirpitz* apparently unaware of their approach. Within a minute, five Tallboys went down but before the results could be seen or the rest of the attacks made, the area was covered with a smokescreen. The Film Lancaster flew directly back to Waddington with no more than inconclusive evidence. The others went back to Yagodnik and thence home later. Two hours afterwards the Mosquito came over Alten Fjord to see what had happened but through fleeting gaps in what was now extensive cloud, the pilot could learn little more than that the ship was still there. Five days later a photograph showed the ship had been damaged but to what extent could not be judged.

In fact the *Tirpitz* had been almost mortally wounded in this complicated and brilliant bomber operation. The Germans estimated it would have taken nine months to repair the ship and they decided not to bother. Instead they took her at a painful six or seven knots from Alten to Tromsö which brought her just within Lancaster 'hotted up' range from Lossiemouth. From there on 12th November 1944 thirty-one Lancasters, as before from 617 and 9 Squadrons, took off for the *Tirpitz* again. They attacked from between 12,850 and 16,000 feet and when they turned for home the battleship was already listing. Shortly afterwards she turned turtle. Of the 1,900 men on board, 1,000 were killed or injured. It cost Bomber Command neither an aircraft nor a life.

Such spectacular triumph, nor all

The German battleship *Tirpitz*. Bottom picture shows upturned hull after Bomber Command's attack

the huge though ill-coordinated bombing offensive, nor even the vast American, British and Russian military operations could, however, yet bring the indomitable Germans and their possessed leader to their knees. On the contrary, at the end of the year when it might have been hoped the war would be over, the Germans launched a counteroffensive through the Ardennes.

On 14th January 1945, General Arnold, the Commanding General of the United States Army Air Forces, wrote to his principal Operational Commander, General Carl Spaatz: 'We have a superiority of at least 5 to 1 now against Germany and yet, in spite of all our hopes, anticipations, dreams and plans, we have as yet not

been able to capitalize to the extent which we should. We may not be able to force capitulation on the Germans by air attacks, but on the other hand, with this tremendous striking power, it would seem to me that we should get much better and much more decisive results than we are getting now. I am not criticizing, because frankly I don't know the answer and what I am now doing is letting my thoughts run wild with the hope that

out of this you may get a glimmer, a light, a new thought, or something which will help us to bring this war to a close sooner.'

These revealing confessions of General Arnold show the frustration and even despondency which pervaded the Allied councils at this juncture in their affairs. The Ardennes offensive which had greatly diverted Allied air power and delayed Eisenhower's plans for advancing into Germany, would soon be contained, but it afforded depressing evidence of continuing German resilience. The war seemed not only to be dragging on endlessly but it was dragging on dangerously, into a new and alarming era of weapon developments. The possibility of the atomic bomb had appeared. The Germans had already produced and launched the V1 pilotless plane and the yet more advanced V2 partly guided missile. Now they were demonstrating a clear lead over the Allies in the development of high speed manned flight. Already they had substantial numbers of jet propelled fighters in operation. And the Germans were fitting breathers to their U-boats, known as Schnorkels, which enabled them to remain much longer submerged and so made them much harder to hunt. Was the Allied command of the air and the sea, so painfully fought for and so convincingly won in 1944, to be reversed in 1945? Could Germany be beaten and Hitler removed in that year? How long would the Allied war efforts endure? At this moment the Russians took the offensive and resumed their rapid advance towards the eastern frontiers of Germany.

From this situation there emerged in the western camp a series of new factors affecting the direction of the Anglo-American bomber forces. Firstly, and on top of the huge effort devoted in December 1944 and January 1945 by the air forces to the restoration of the military situation following the Ardennes offensive, there was the defensive consideration that attacks on German fighter aircraft production and U-boat targets would have to be resumed. Secondly, there was the feeling that whether the war could be quickly brought to an end or not depended more upon the Russian advance than anything else and that, therefore, ways of assisting the Red Army through bombing should be examined. Thirdly, there was the feeling, hinted at by General Arnold and also much canvassed by General Marshall, the Chief of the United States Army Staff, that some new, dramatic and decisive use for the heavy bombers should be sought in an attempt to break out of the frustrations of December and January. Fourthly, there were the surviving oil and transport plans which Portal and Tedder continued firmly to believe must have their priorities preserved as, in spite of all the confusing circumstances, the best means of getting on with winning the war open to the bombers.

The 'tremendous striking power' to which Arnold had referred in his letter to Spaatz, now amounted, without reckoning the large tactical air forces, to an operational strength of not much less than 4,000 bombers. The Eighth Air Force in January 1945 frequently despatched 1,500 bombers on operations in a day and the Fifteenth Air Force, though smaller, achieved a somewhat higher standard of accuracy than the Eighth. Neither force, however, had really come to terms with the European climate and especially that which prevailed in the winter months. During January, for example, eighty per cent of the Eighth and Fifteenth Air Force bombing attacks were made on radar indications from above cloud. In such attacks the average circular error of the Eighth Air Force was about two miles in diameter and that of the Fifteenth Air Force about one.

Under such conditions and generally in better weather too, Bomber Command normally achieved much more accurate results. Depending less on formation tactics, which in any case it lacked the skill to achieve in refined form, there was in Bomber Command, both in area and precision attacks, more individual aiming and less pattern bombing, though the latter was sometimes used by the British in daylight attacks guided by Oboe and a new radar aid,GH. Bomber Command also continued to carry much more destructive loads than the American Fortresses and Liberators. Not only was the average bomb lift of a British bomber, at around 8,000lbs, more than twice the American average, but the big bombs themselves including now the ten ton Grandslam were of special importance in all the really formidable tasks such as the permanent wrecking of oil plants, the destruction of major viaducts, such as that at Bielefeld, the breaching of canal banks and the sinking of battleships or the penetration of railway tunnels or concrete protected U-boat pens.

Bomber Command, however, was now substantially inferior in numbers to the American forces. In January 1945 the average daily strength ready for operations in Bomber Command with crews was 1,420. By April it had risen to 1,609. This force nevertheless discharged month by month in 1945 approximately the same bomb tonnage as the Eighth Air Force. Between January and May Bomber Command dropped 181,740 tons and the Eighth Air Force 188,573 tons, (long tons) though it must be noted that these totals are the product of the exact addition of necessarily approximate figures.

In its operations, Bomber Command, however, continued to owe much to the United States. Not only, for example, were many of the Merlin engines which powered most of its Lancasters, many of its Halifaxes and all its Mosquitoes, built under licence in America, but its now very low casualties bore constant testimony to the effectiveness of the command of the air which, above all other considerations, was due to American Fortress and Liberator bombers and American Mustang, Thunderbolt and Lightning fighters. Indeed, from the 67,483 sorties flown by Bomber Command in 1945 before VE-Day only 608 failed to return.

This effort, in terms of the tonnages of bombs dropped, was distributed between area attacks on cities which absorbed about a third, oil targets about a quarter, transportation about fifteen per cent, direct military targets such as troops and fortifications about fourteen per cent, naval targets about six per cent, and the rest a little over one per cent. The American effort showed a larger concentration on transportation and a lesser one on cities which in any case were not by the Americans categorised under that heading, but on the whole their distribution corresponded broadly to that of Bomber Command and in this final phase the operations were more in the nature of a combined bomber offensive than ever before.

Despite distractions, second thoughts and bright ideas there was a heavy and effective concentration on the oil plan, which by early April was brought to complete fruition. The Fifteenth Air Force had made an important contribution, at the outset by attacking Ploesti and subsequently by concentrating against Austrian, Hungarian and south German targets. The crux of the campaign was, however, borne by the Eighth Air Force and Bomber Command and the synthetic oil plants were, of course, the most important targets. In these operations between May 1944 and April 1945 forty-two plants were attacked by Bomber Command, which aimed more than 63,000 tons of bombs at them, and the Eighth Air Force which aimed over 45,000 tons.

By February most and by March all the major oil plants had been completely destroyed and only a few minor benzol producers were left to supplement diminishing natural

The German naval base at Kiel, 1945

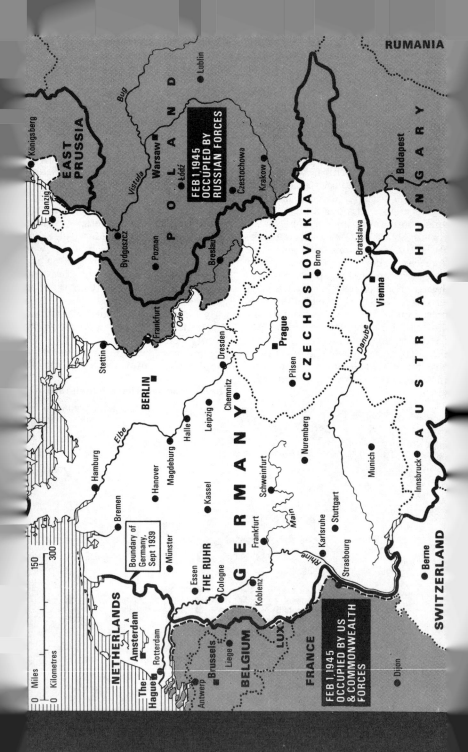

RUMANIA

EAST PRUSSIA

Königsberg

Danzig

Bug

Lublin

POLAND

Warsaw

Vistula

Łódź

Czestochowa

Krakow

FEB 1,1945
OCCUPIED BY
RUSSIAN FORCES

Bydgoszcz

Poznan

Breslau

Budapest

H U N G A R Y

Oder

Frankfurt

Bratislava

Brno

C Z E C H O S L O V A K I A

Vienna

A U S T R I A

Stettin

Prague

BERLIN

Dresden

Pilsen

Danube

Chemnitz

Elbe

Leipzig

Halle

Nuremberg

Magdeburg

G E R M A N Y

Innsbruck

Hamburg

Hanover

Kassel

Schweinfurt

Munich

Bremen

Frankfurt

Main

Stuttgart

Münster

Karlsruhe

Boundary of
Germany,
Sept 1939

Essen

Cologne

Koblenz

THE RUHR

Rhine

Strasbourg

Berne

SWITZERLAND

150

300

Miles

Kilometres

NETHERLANDS

Amsterdam

Rotterdam

The
Hague

Antwerp

Brussels

Liège

BELGIUM

LUX.

F R A N C E

Dijon

0

FEB 1,1945
OCCUPIED BY US
& COMMONWEALTH
FORCES

supplies from Hungary. The German army and air forces were now dependent on what stocks remained in the few depots which had not yet been bombed. After April, further major military and air operations were impossible for Germany owing to the shortage of fuel. If late in its achievement, the result was ultimately and completely decisive in its effect.

Transport bombing had produced a scarcely less decisive effect. By 24th March 1945 the Ruhr had been completely cut off from the rest of Germany by a bombing campaign in which the tactical air forces, British and American, greatly aided the efforts of the heavy bombers, but this achievement came only a week before the area was in any case surrounded by the Allied armies. Even so, German industry had already suffered severely from the effects of the earlier partial isolation of the Ruhr and by the time the Ruhr was lost the general attack on communications was producing an industrial, military and even administrative seizure in many parts of the country.

As in the case of the oil campaign, the absolute bombing results were more or less overtaken by the advance of the armies from the west and the east but these advances, of course, themselves owed a great deal to the strategic campaigns against oil and transport. There were also, however, other ways in which the British and American Air Staffs sought to speed up the date of military victory. In particular, at the beginning of the year when they were suffering so grievously from a sense of frustration and when the main hope of early victory seemed to turn upon the Russian offensive, which began in the middle of January, attention had been focussed upon what the bombing could do to help the Russians. In this way the earlier idea of a plan known as Thunderclap developed a new application.

Thunderclap, it will be remembered, envisaged a state in which the German armies had been virtually defeated in the field and the Allies were delicately poised between the possibility of receiving an organised surrender and having to deal with an outbreak of anarchy and underground warfare. In such a situation it had been thought a sudden pulverising blow from the air, probably against Berlin, might avail to bring the German authorities to the state of mind in which they would make an organised surrender and the German people to the condition in which they would accept it.

Towards the end of January the thought occurred that this plan, associated with attacks on communications behind the German eastern front, might be an effective way of enabling the bombers to contribute to a speeding up of the Russian advance. The attacks on Berlin would be designed to convince the Germans that further resistance would be hopeless and very costly. The attacks on communications would have the object of delaying the arrival of their troops at the points of the Russian advance. There was also the expectation that Berlin would be packed with refugees fleeing before the Russians and that heavy bombing would, therefore, at the critical moment produce a severe administrative problem for the Germans. Finally, there was the belief that it would be desirable to demonstrate to the Russians that the British and Americans were able and willing to afford active assistance to their operations.

All this was clear enough and the idea too gave some expression to the pronounced feeling that something drastic ought to be done out of the ordinary to try to hurry the war on and speed up the approach of its end. From here on, however, the story becomes somewhat more confused and since the development and ultimate execution of the plan have left in some quarters a question mark against the conduct of the British and Americans and since, too, considerable mis-

Dresden

understanding and misrepresentation have survived, it may be as well to trace it in some detail.

On the evening of 25th January 1945, the Deputy Chief of the Air Staff, Sir Norman Bottomley, telephoned Harris to inform him of the development of the plans and to discuss them with him. Harris said he already had in mind the idea of attacking Berlin and he suggested that this should be supplemented by attacks of a similar nature and simultaneous timing against Chemnitz, Leipzig and Dresden. Like Berlin, these towns might well also be congested with refugees fleeing before the Russians and they also were focal points in the German communications system leading to the eastern front. Bottomley reported this conversation to his Chief, Portal, the next day and pointed out that, as the attacks on Berlin were to be on such a massive scale, General Spaatz should be brought in on them.

Portal was at this time preparing to leave for Malta en route with the Prime Minister for the Conference of the Grand Alliance which was to be held under Russian auspices at Yalta and he already had another urgent reason for considering how, if at all, bombing policy should be adapted to help the Russians. On the evening before, Mr Churchill, possibly with the question in mind of how his talks with Stalin would go, asked the Secretary of State for Air, Sir Archibald Sinclair, what plans there were for attacking the Germans from the air in their retreat from Breslau. At least that was what Sinclair thought he had been asked.

Thus, on 26th January, Portal gave his opinion as to what should be done. He was against really massive operations over Berlin. He thought the results would not be decisive and he feared that the bomber casualties would be high. Nor was he in favour of any substantial diversion of the bombing effort on to communications leading to the eastern front. He did not think it would be worth while. He thought it much more worth while to maintain the highest priority for attacks upon German oil production. All the same he believed it would be desirable to make one big attack on Berlin and also to bomb Dresden, Leipzig, Chemnitz 'or any other cities where a severe blitz will not only cause confusion in the evacuation from the east but will also hamper the movement of troops from the west'.

Accordingly, also on 26th January, Sinclair addressed a minute to the Prime Minister dealing with the question raised on the previous evening. He said that the targets which the Germans would offer in a massive retreat towards Berlin and Dresden could best be exploited by tactical air forces and that this should be exploited by Russian ground strafing fighters. He saw little hope of British and American heavy bombers intervening in this tactical sphere especially as they would not have the means of knowing exactly where the Germans ended and the Russians began. He then explained the view that the best use of the heavy bombers was to maintain the oil campaign and that this would benefit not only the western alliance but also the Russians. All the same, when the weather was unsuitable for oil operations, there might, Sinclair explained, be opportunities for bombing Berlin 'and other cities in eastern Germany such as Leipzig, Dresden and Chemnitz, which are not only the administrative centres controlling the military and civilian movements but are also the main communications centres through which the bulk of the traffic moves'. Sinclair's minute ended with the news that the possibility of such attacks being carried out on a scale sufficient to have a critical effect on the situation in eastern Germany was 'under examination'.

This was not enough for the Prime Minister, who clearly thought the time had come, not for further discussion, but for immediate decision. He told Sinclair at once that he was not concerned with the tactical harassing of the Germans in their retreat on the eastern front. He wanted to know 'whether Berlin, and no doubt other large cities in east Germany, should not now be considered especially attractive targets'. He was glad this question was 'under examination'. But, he concluded, 'Pray report to me tomorrow what is going to be done'.

Thus the situation was once more clarified. On 27th January without further ado, Bottomley, formally and on behalf of the Air Staff, directed Harris, as soon as moon and weather conditions permitted, to make 'one big attack on Berlin and related attacks on Dresden, Leipzig, Chemnitz' or other suitable cities. Sinclair at once informed Churchill that this had been done. He added that Harris had undertaken to attempt the operations as soon as the moon waned and the weather was right. This, Sinclair warned the Prime Minister, was unlikely to be before about 4th February. Before he left for Malta, Portal and Bottomley discussed the priorities with Spaatz and shortly afterwards Bottomley and Spaatz conferred with Tedder. On 31st January Bottomley was able to let Portal, now in Malta, know they they had agreed upon the priorities as firstly the oil plan, secondly, the bombing of Berlin, Leipzig, Dresden and associated cities, thirdly, communications leading to the eastern and western fronts, fourthly, jet aircraft plants and a marginal effort for tank factories. Spaatz had already given the Eighth Air Force orders to initiate the plan by attacking Berlin. In view of the speed of the Russian advance it was felt the Russians should now be informed of these plans.

At Yalta, there was indeed some discussion of these matters. In a memorandum which the Deputy Chief of Staff of the Red Army tabled on 4th February, the Russians asked that their Western Allies should seek to prevent the Germans from moving troops from the western front, from Norway and Italy to their own front 'by air attacks against communications' and in particular they asked that the bombing should 'paralyse the centres: Berlin and Leipzig'.

Meanwhile, on 3rd February the plan sprang into action. Nearly 1,000 Fortresses of the American Eighth Air Force arrived over Berlin in clear weather and from between 24,000 and 27,000 feet delivered an extremely damaging attack upon the administrative centre of the city. The casualties suffered by the Berliners were unusually high and as many as 25,000 may have been killed. On 6th February, Eighth Air Force attacks were made on Magdeburg and Chemnitz in each case to the tune of nearly 800 tons of bombs. On the night of 13th February, Bomber Command despatched just over 800 aircraft in two waves to Dresden. The flying conditions proved to be perfect. The German opposition en route and over the target proved to be nil. The concentration and accuracy of the attack therefore proved to be exceptional and the damage inflicted unprecedented. In daylight on 14th February, 400 Eighth Air Force bombers attacked the already devastated city and that night Bomber Command attacked Chemnitz in what proved to be a much less effective operation. The Eighth Air Force gave further expression to the plan in more massive daylight attacks including another on Berlin on 26th February and two more on Dresden on 2nd March and 17th April.

Terrific and terrible destruction was caused. By far the greatest ordeal fell on Dresden during the Bomber Command night attack which produced fire-storms, ruin and death on a scale reminiscent of what had happened to Hamburg in July and August 1943 and a portent of what was to come to Tokyo from incendiary and Hiroshima and Nagasaki from atomic bombs.

Night take-off: Lancaster

Summary and verdict

At the end of the war public opinion turned away from bombing which, especially in Britain, it had once so strongly supported. It was not just a question of people being tired of war and disgusted by its horrors. There seemed to be a special feeling of outrage about bombing and even a quarter of a century later it is the tragedies and suffering caused by bombing which seem to offend the memory or the impression more than the other horrors of the 20th Century, such as the German concentration camps or the Russian Revolution or the slaughter of the infantry in the First World War or the fate of prisoners who fell into Japanese hands in the Second.

Strategic bombing, which by its very nature must fall upon the heart of nations, is indeed a terrible thing to witness or even to contemplate and the extension of its capacity by the introduction and use of atomic weapons in the closing stages of the war against Japan make its future application a virtually unthinkable prospect. But whatever the future may hold will not change the content of the past and the place of strategic bombing in the Second World War deserves to be coolly appraised.

The brunt of the bombing in the Second World War was borne by the criminal nations, Germany and Japan, criminal in the sense that, despite the arguments and qualifications, it was they and not the British, the French, the Americans or the Russians who caused the war. Naturally it would have been better for the Germans and the Japanese if bombing had been restricted to the tactical sphere and used only in direct support of armies and navies. If this had been so, their own homelands would have escaped the awful destruction which fell on them and their initially much superior forces would have had at least a much enhanced prospect of winning the war.

When the Germans arrived on the Channel coast in 1940 there were not in England many scruples about bombing their cities. After the Japanese had struck down the American fleet at Pearl Harbor in 1941, there were not many Americans who would have withheld a salute from General Doolittle who led the first bombing attack on Tokyo. When the Russians were fighting at the approaches to Moscow, Leningrad or Stalingrad for their very existence, there were perhaps not many who would have condemned Stalin for praising Britain's area attacks on Berlin. The first essential step in a cool appraisal of bombing is to recognise it in its true historical context.

There is, however, the consideration that many appraisals made of strategic bombing indicate that it was ineffective and therefore to that extent wanton in the sense that it caused suffering and death without contributing to victory. The argument is often heard that Britain and America would have done better not to develop a long range bomber effort but to devote their air potential to the maritime war or the land battle. And by better is often meant not only strategically better but morally better too. A slightly more tolerant variant of the same argument which also often appears is that strategic bombing was not of itself wanton but that the particular application which it developed was. In particular, it is sometimes suggested, bombing should have been restricted to 'military objectives'. Civilian populations should not have been attacked. Thus, the implication is, the war-winning virtues of bombing could have been secured and the moral penalties avoided.

If in fact Britain and America had failed to build up strategic bombing forces and had devoted all their efforts to military and maritime purposes it is arguable that the victories which they won in North Africa might possibly have been won more easily and it is also arguable that victory in the Battle of the Atlantic might have come a little earlier and more convincingly. Neither thesis however is open to proof. If the Allies had not had Bomber Command and the United States Strategic Air Forces in Europe, it by no means follows that they would necessarily have had effective military and maritime air forces. In any case, tremendous contributions to the land battle and the war at sea were made by Bomber Command and the American Strategic Air Forces. If, however, these forces had not been built up then it can categorically be established that the war effort against Germany would have been denied three actual aspects. Firstly, after Dunkirk Britain would have had no means whatsoever of bringing to bear directly against Germany any war making of any kind, unless she had been prepared to land Commando units on German territory. In such circumstances it may be asked if Britain's fighting morale could have been maintained. As it was, Bomber Command, in its continuing attacks on Germany from May 1940 to May 1945 provided the element of direct attack and the hope of decisive result throughout the war.

Secondly, it has to be recognised that without the strategic air offensive the battle for command of the air, which was fought and won largely through the agency of American day bombing and long range fighters in February and March 1944, could not have been fought and won as it was over Germany. Since there can be no doubt that this battle for the command of the air was one of the decisive battles of the war in the sense that it made possible the Normandy landings and the effective phase of the strategic air offensive alike, the results of it not

having been fought and won are incalculable. They would indeed, in all probability have changed the whole course and duration of the war.

Thirdly, if the strategic air offensive had not been built up over the years into the effective instrument of destruction which it became by 1944, the French railway campaign of March–June 1944, the oil campaign of May 1944–April 1945 and the transportation campaign of the same period could not have been undertaken. In these circumstances, it is perfectly reasonable to wonder if Eisenhower's armies, which found the going hard and slow enough as it was, would ever have got inshore from Normandy and, if they had, across France and into the heart of Germany.

These decisive operations of strategic air power were, however, all of a selective nature. The battle for air superiority over Germany was fought over an attack by bombers on selected aspects of the German war economy, chiefly the aircraft industry. The railway, oil and transportation campaigns were selective as opposed to general targets. All involved attack on towns and therefore civilians since marshalling yards, for example, and oil plants were often in built up urban areas, but the attacks were nevertheless aimed at the installations as opposed to the people. The civilians killed were therefore killed incidentally, as opposed to deliberately. In the area attacks on the centres of the main German cities the same could not be said with truth. Here the aiming points were usually chosen to produce the greatest general dislocation of the city in question. The particular objects were to dehouse the people and destroy the public amenities and services such as water, gas, electricity and transport. Inevitably this meant aiming at the people themselves. Area bombing was a direct attack upon the German people.

Lancasters of 50 Squadron

A kill for German fighters

The American bomber forces, though they later openly adopted the policy of general area attack against Japanese cities, and though they frequently, both by accident and on purpose, carried out general area attacks on German cities, including Berlin and Dresden, never overtly adopted the policy of general area bombing against Germany. They always maintained the view that the targets were marshalling yards or factories which happened to be within cities. The overt policy of area bombing of Germany was therefore a British preserve and it arose and was maintained for two principal reasons. Firstly, in the initial stages of the campaign it became probable and then certain that in the most accurate attacks of which it was capable, Bomber Command could not, under normal circumstances, profitably aim at anything less than a whole town centre. In other words, if it aimed at an object in open country or at sea, the overwhelming proportion of its effort would fall harmlessly in fields or in the water. If, on the other hand, it aimed at the centres of cities, the greater proportion of its effort would eventually do damage of some kind to Germany. When there was nothing else available with which to damage Germany, this consideration had a not unreasonable attraction especially as, with perhaps less excuse, the Germans had adopted the same policy over London, Coventry, Birmingham, Manchester, Hull, Glasgow, Plymouth and other cities.

The second reason supporting the idea of area bombing was the evident fallibility of intelligence. Attacks on particular targets such as the ball bearing plants at Schweinfurt, the Möhne Dam and so on were liable to produce very disappointing results not because they failed but because the German war effort was far less dependent upon them than had been supposed. Whole cities, however, could not be moved underground, otherwise concealed or, in the long run, done without. General attack was less dependent upon accurate intelligence than was selective attack. This was a consideration which maintained its force after the time, in 1944, when at least on many occasions, Bomber Command had an operational choice between area and precision attack, that is when it had, through the development of techniques and the security of command of the air, the ability to hit not just cities but particular installations. This was the basis of the disagreement between Portal and Harris which became so pronounced in October 1944 and the following months. Even so, there were many surviving occasions when a major area attack still seemed to most of those directing the strategy of the war, to be the best policy available. Such an occasion was that which led to the destruction of Dresden in February 1945.

Area bombing in general and the attacks on Dresden in particular, have in the light of post-war investigation come in for a bad press. This, no doubt, is largely due to the facts that area bombing produced strategic results which were disappointing and certainly markedly less effective than the selective attacks, and that the destruction of Dresden was not only excessive but possibly, by the time that it occurred, unnecessary.

This, however, is not to say, as it is often claimed, that area bombing was wholly ineffective. What can be established is this: despite area bombing the production of German armaments of all kinds continued to rise until July 1944 and that this production was sufficient to maintain truly formidable German war operations in Russia, the Middle East, Italy and France. Secondly, however depressed, alarmed or terrorised the German people may have been by the attacks to which they were subjected, their national morale and civil obedience was broadly maintained and Hitler, up to almost the end, continued to exact a fanatical loyalty from the masses. Thirdly, area bombing, unlike the American attacks, did not lead to

a decisive battle with the German air force and so make a contribution to the winning of the command of the air. This was because area bombing depended upon the evasion of the enemy air force and offered no scope for the destruction of it. Night bombers could, if they were fortunate, occasionally shoot down night fighters, but, as a regular feature, the contest usually went the other way and the bombers' main hope of survival was to steer clear as best they could of the opposition. This was the striking contrast to what eventually became possible for the day bombers of General Spaatz's American forces. Their aim became the stirring up of the German fighters so that their own fighters could get in among them. Finally it has to be reckoned that the comparative failure of area bombing, relative to other forms of attack, was not due simply to failure to concentrate enough upon it and to keep it up long enough. Area bombing depended, on the British side, upon the success of evasive measures and, on the German side, upon the power of recovery, repair, rescue and reconstruction. Thus the struggle fluctuated with each technical innovation such as window, which helped the bombers to evade the fighters, and such as the 'running commentary' system which enabled the German fighters largely to neutralise 'window'; and also upon the development of relief measures in the German cities. Over the campaign as a whole it becomes quite evident that the German capacity to absorb the growing destruction inflicted by Bomber Command grew at a greater rate than Bomber Command's ability to contain the casualties inflicted upon it, mainly by the German night fighter force. The outcome of the Battle of Berlin in March 1944 made it abundantly evident that a further intensification of the campaign would ruin not Germany but Bomber Command.

So there is substance in the belief that area bombing, judged relatively, was ineffective. It was not, however, wholly ineffective, nor for much of the war was there any alternative to it either for the British or the Americans, if a bombing offensive was to be maintained at all. Nor of course would the final achievements of the bombing forces have been possible without the preceding endeavours. Great fighting forces cannot be conjured up at the moments of need without the prior establishment of operational experience and fighting morale. As for the attack on Dresden, it was really a case of too much and too late. When the attack was planned there were solid and convincing reasons for undertaking it. By the time it was carried out these reasons were on a less firm foundation. That, however, was not apparent at the time. The mistake had been made before of assuming the war was on the point of being won. The reward had been the Ardennes offensive. Nevertheless, the attacks made, and particularly Bomber Command's night operation, did produce gross over-bombing. This too, however, could not be foreseen. A force of about 800 bombers had never before in a single night produced such an effect as occurred in Dresden. Indeed, a night later a similar force, operating in the same area of Germany, produced a far less impressive result. The Dresden result was due to a combination of perfect weather, perfect visibility and the curious circumstance that the Germans offered no opposition whatsoever.

Though some have claimed to know the number of men, women and children killed in this Dresden attack, the fact remains that it is impossible to establish it with certainty or precision. Even the estimates which purport to be historical rather than hysterical are frequently revised and do not rest on historical evidence. In truth, all that can be said is that the casualties were appalling and may well have exceeded the 50,000 or so killed in the Battle of Hamburg.

Dreadful as this was, and more dreadful as it now seems to a world passing, mercifully, through a more tranquil period in which Hitler is hardly more than an evil memory, it has to be recognised that the Dresden attack, and its follow-up was meant to constitute a blow of shattering force, devastating effect and demoralising consequence for any surviving German war plans. It is hard to believe and impossible to prove that the bombing of Dresden did not have a marked effect upon the speed at which German resistance disintegrated. It may thus be reckoned at best an effective strategic method of hastening the date at which relief could be brought to those still hanging on in the concentration camps and at which the heat could be turned on to Japan. At worst it was no more than an attempt to achieve those aims and to relieve the war-weary nations of the Grand Alliance of the hideous military commitment with which Germany had saddled them.

In summary and in verdict it may be said of the strategic air offensive that it succeeded to the extent that it made a decisive and indispensable contribution to victory. This was decisive in the sense that it played a vital role in achieving the command of the air. This in turn made possible a change in the course of the war and, through this achievement and also through the destruction of communications in France, it made a contribution to Overlord without which that undertaking must have had a high chance of failure. Moreover, in the final phase of the war, mainly through the oil and transportation campaigns, but also partly through area attacks on cities, it resulted in the paralysis of Germany's industrial and administrative base and so greatly facilitated her total defeat by the Soviet armies from the east and the Anglo-American ones from the west. These results were indispensable both in the sense that without them the whole course of the war would have been different and in that they could not have been achieved by any other force such as, for example, the various brands of tactical air power which the Germans, Russians and Japanese developed exclusively and the British and Americans in relation to strategic air power.

Impressive and important as these results were, they were by no means the best which, theoretically at least, might have been achieved. The shortfall of strategic bombing for much of the war, and it was not until 1944 that really major results were achieved, was primarily due to two lacks, lack of destructive power and lack of command of the air. The destructive power needed to achieve decisive results proved to be enormously greater than estimated beforehand. This was partly due to the extraordinary stoicism, loyalty and capacity for work under fire of the German people and partly due to the great difficulty, again much greater than foreseen, of carrying out accurate bombing under war conditions. This last difficulty arose directly from the lack of command of the air which characterised the greater part in time of the strategic air offensive. German fighters made massive day bombing impossible for Bomber Command until the second half of 1944 and so set them the problem of finding targets at night. For the Eighth Air Force they dictated the tactic of massed formations which allowed only 'pattern' bombing to be adopted. Moreover, the German fighter force imposed another critical handicap; it prevented systematic concentration and repeat bombing of the priority targets. The bombers had to spread the defences by spreading the attacks. This was particularly shown on the morrow of the American attack on the ball bearing plants at Schweinfurt in October 1943 and in the closing stages of the Battle of Berlin in February and March 1944. After the command of the air had been won, by day in April 1944 and by night in August 1944, the limiting factors remaining became the weather, the German ground defences and defects in the system of high command. Of these, the last was the least inevitable and the most serious. Suffice it to say that those who bore the responsibility at the time had neither the indications of previous history which were available to their naval and military colleagues, nor the hindsight of those, including the present author, who offer their historical appraisals.

Of the two main forces involved, the British Bomber Command not only fought the longer campaign but also generated by far the greater destructive power. The American Eighth Air Force, however, made by far the greater contribution to the winning of the command of the air. Harris, the Commander-in-Chief of Bomber Command, will perhaps go down in history as a giant among the leaders of men. He gave Bomber Command the courage to surmount its ordeals, he gave Churchill the reason to keep Bomber Command in being and he gave Arnold the evidence to make his case for an American strategic air offensive. Spaatz, the Commanding General of the United States Strategic Air Forces in Europe, deserves a different laurel. He, more than any other air commander, seized upon the need and the method to win the command of the air. He got his forces into a critical action and despite distractions and even directives he kept them in that action until a decisive outcome had been achieved. No doubt, unpremeditated opportunism played a big part in Spaatz's achievement. No doubt too he owed much to superlative subordinate commanders, and especially General Kepner of the Eighth Fighter Command, but the chief credit for victory must go, as blame for defeat would also have done, to the top commander – in this case, Spaatz. Nor in war, which is not a game of chess, should intellectual reasoning be put at a premium even in the highest operational commanders; intuitive judgment, or, as Napoleon might have put it, luck, is a much more important quality.

Bibliography

The Strategic Air Offensive against Germany 1939-1945 Sir Charles Webster and Noble Frankland (HMSO, London, 4 vols)

The Army Air Forces in World War II W L Craven and J L Cate (Ed) (Chicago, 7 vols)

The Bombing Offensive against Germany Noble Frankland (Faber, London)

Bomber Offensive Marshal of the Royal Air Force Sir Arthur Harris (Collins, London)

The Luftwaffe War Diaries Cajus Bekker (Macdonald, London. Doubleday, New York)

The Bombing of Germany Hans Rumpf (Frederick Muller, London. Holt, Rinehart and Winston, New York)

The First and the Last Adolph Galland (Methuen, London. Holt, Rinehart and Winston, New York)

The Dam Busters Paul Brickhill (Evans Brothers, London. Norton, New York)